# The Big Book of Life Excuses

## ... and the Solution!

*Neil James Thompson*
**The Motorbiking
Motivator**

# The Big Book of Life Excuses
## ... and the Solution!

## By Neil James Thompson

ISBN 978-1-84914-661-6

Published by Nidrick Publishing 2015

www.neiljamesthompson.com

Printed in the UK by Completely Novel.

www.neiljamesthompson.com

# A 5-step formula for an excuse-free life

## A book full of 'red diamonds' of wisdom

### This book is for you if...

- You want to become too powerful for excuse-making.
- You want to create balance-awareness in your life.
- You want to accept, like and be proud of who you are.
- You want to have more money.
- You want to have more friends.
- You want to have a mind and a voice of your own.
- You want to create a winning attitude.
- You want to have more fun.
- You want to significantly improve your fitness levels.
- You want to live your life from a higher place.
- You want freedom.

Surrey Motivation

# Contents

## Chapter 1

## Chapter 2

# Chapter 3

# Chapter 4

# Chapter 5

# Chapter 6

# Chapter 7

## Neil's 'Enlightenment' Of Quotations . . . . . . . . . . . . . . . 215

# Foreword

## *by George Daplyn*

I've known Neil for a number of years through our mutual interest in personal development and motorbikes. During this time I have witnessed him deliver powerful motivational speeches, inspiring and uplifting his audiences with warmth, charm and charisma.

I was delighted to have been invited to attend the incredibly successful, first ever Life Excuses seminar, held on October 27th 2013 at the Farnham House Hotel in Surrey. The event was truly inspirational, featuring personal development, music and humour. It gives me equal pleasure now to be invited to write the foreword for this excellent book, which presents Neil's personal philosophy of what's needed to become an excuse-free student of success – and so creating a stronger version of you.

The fact that you're reading this book tells me that you're probably someone who recognises that you haven't reached your true potential, and are looking for practical suggestions to correct this. The answers can be found here, because if you're hungry for an excuse-free life where you long to feast on the good stuff, then the strategies in this book will lead you straight to the top table. It teaches you how to live respectfully in all areas of your life, and to move forward with purpose. It offers a beacon of hope, for those who feel that they're being bent double by the challenging winds of life; a guiding light on the road to excellence, if you like, in an easy-to-read, step-by-step fashion that can be followed exactly, or dipped into at selected places for creating results specific to your needs.

It's a book about raising the standards, about moving away from the gunk of life, so if you're ready to release the brakes and get moving towards a more fulfilling future then 'The Big Book of Life Excuses ... and the Solution!' offers the ideal road map.

With a skilful mix of positive strategies, original quotations, true stories and hilarious illustrations this book is a joy to read – don't just buy it and put it on the shelf – instead, keep it by your bedside as a reference manual while you incorporate its teachings into your life.

*George Daplyn*

# A Statement of
# Power
# and Purpose

*My essence is divine spirit and I must listen to the voice of my soul, the voice of truth; the sole director of my destiny.*

*The life force within me, the energy of my being propels me ever forward towards the manifestation of my dream. No man but I has the power of decision over which path I choose through life. I unleash the passion of my purpose by wilfully engaging the full fury of any storm with defiance – undaunted by thunder and lightning, unmoved by the heavy rain that can never dampen nor extinguish the fire that burns inside my heart.*

*I am a warrior, with a mind of resourcefulness and strength, born from inner knowledge and wisdom, sent to slay mediocrity and embrace excellence. I am the owner of my thoughts, the owner of my life ... and therefore ... I am the master of my fate!*

*Neil James Thompson*
**The Motorbiking Motivator**

www.neiljamesthompson.com

# About Neil

**Neil James Thompson, the Motorbiking Motivator is a personal development author, songwriter, entrepreneur and visionary thinker.** He's had a passion for helping people make the most of their lives for many, many years. His interest in personal development can be traced back to 1989 where he chanced to read some articles from health magazines on the mind–body approach to fitness. He still has these articles to this day as testament to the progress he's made with his own journey. It was his learning and continual studying that led him to write this book – a lifestyle book with personality that offers up strategies and disciplines for excuse-busting that really do work, if you take the time to implement them into your life.

As a long-time member of the Toastmasters International public speaking organisation he's become a popular and charismatic presenter of his ideas, using humour and storytelling to deliver his message. Based in Guildford in Surrey, England he's helped many organisations and individuals to maximise their true potential by sharing his personal success philosophy with them.

He also has over thirty years' experience in writing contemporary music and often uses this to give his seminars a very personal and unique flavour.

# Introduction

**Hi, I'm Neil James Thompson. Welcome to 'The Big Book of Life Excuses ... and the Solution!'**

If you've ever been interested in creating an excuse-free life of greater happiness, contentment and fulfilment then this book is definitely for you.

It answers the big questions, such as: "How do we go from being excuse-makers to life-makers?" "How do we go from lower ground to higher ground, from the dead zone to the land of the truly living?" "How do we make our lives a tapestry of tremendous times – a sumptuous banquet rather than a scramble for the crumbs?"

It presents to you the Positive Life-Balance Code: a platform for balance-awareness as a series of strategies based on disciplines that, once implemented into your everyday life, becomes the solution to excuse-making. In brief, it's about creating an excuse-busting lifestyle!

One of the important things I've learnt through personal experience is how important it's for us to take full responsibility for everything that happens to us. When we do this, we know that we've finally grown up; we're not children anymore. In other words, if we're serious about changing some aspect of our lives that we're not happy with, we have to implement the strategies of change to get the results that we want ... we have to do the work!

It was the realisation that we're basically, with the universe, the co-authors and co-creators of every success and failure that occurs in our lives, by the choices and decisions we make, and it was this that made me so curious about the science of personal development. As I contemplated the twists and turns of my own life my curiosity grew and the more convinced I became that a positive life lived to the full was the only way to go.

The opposite only guarantees us anxiety, stress, pain and downright unhappiness ... and who wants a lifetime of that?

It became increasingly clear to me that we needed a formula to take us from a weak, excuse-making mindset to a more powerful, resourceful and wealthy mindset, and this was the key to success and achievement and to being the best that we can be: a simple concept but with the potential to make such a difference to our lives. It was clear that excuses stopped once we'd created that more resourceful state of mind, because resourcefulness, with its raised vibration, gives us that important facility of 'rational clarity'... the ability to see reality in a brighter and clearer light ... to see it as it is rather than as a distorted, inaccurate, sometimes irrational version created by past experiences and leading to excuse-making and subsequent inaction.

Many people suffer from an unresourceful mindset. It becomes a habit, keeping them out of sync with progress by hanging on to yesterday's hurts and pains. Too many people spend too much time reliving past failures, and these poisonous memories, if left unhealed, can become like a ball and chain being dragged along behind them. The reality is that no failure should be seen as a disaster; instead, they should be viewed as stepping stones to success.

Within all of us lie hidden powers that can be used to transform our lives from ordinary to extraordinary; and by gently refocusing our inner vision and revising our expectations one small step at a time, by following the strategies in this book and introducing new positive daily disciplines, we can create a much bigger and better version of ourselves. Then, with 'rational clarity' as mentioned above, we can move forward to claim a rich and rewarding life full of success and abundance ... and, above all, happiness!

# "If you're thinking negative thoughts about past upsets and hurts – then you're not busy enough working on your dreams."

Now, I'm not going to tell you that you can have a perfect life and get everything you want because I don't think that would be possible for anyone; however, one thing that's for sure is that you can have an awful lot more than you're currently experiencing ... and when I say more, I'm not just talking about more money, I'm talking about more meaningful relationships, greater achievements, more confidence, more energy, more fun, more love and greater happiness ... and yes, OK, more money too!

These amazing pay-offs are what makes me so incredibly passionate about 'excuse-stomping' and why I decided to write this book. I certainly can't promise you miracles, but I do believe that by following the ideas and strategies outlined here and by incorporating these into your awareness, you'll be giving yourself a great new foundation for the rest of your journey through life.

I strongly believe, though, that most people struggle with positive intention because they're just not sure how to go about implementing it into their lives; they may have an idea but they lack direction and tenacity – they don't have a definite road map, so they get lost en route. With this book that map is now in your hands.

Creating a life free of excuses is a continual work-in-progress. It would be wrong to aim for a destination called 'perfect life-balance' for no such place exists – The Positive Life-Balance Code as a solution to excuse-making and a strategy for balance-awareness is merely a compass for your journey.

By investing in this product you have taken a bold step towards becoming a student of success ... a new door has opened up in your life: walk through and don't look back ... I wish you well!

**www.neiljamesthompson.com**

# The Author's Guide To Using This Book

I recommend first of all reading this book in its entirety to get the 'lie of the land' before turning to the Quick Start on **page 206** to begin implementing the disciplines of the PLB Code into your life. The QS gives you an easy single-step process for getting started.

Be determined, be persistent, and be consistent when bringing these first simple steps into your awareness. Ideally, allow 14 days of non-stop practice to really get in-the-groove with them. This should be long enough to begin seeing tangible results.

The next step will be to turn to the Action Invitations at the end of each of the five PLB Code chapters (chapters 2 – 6) and begin gradually introducing more daily disciplines into your routine. Anytime you feel you may be slipping in a particular area, dip back into the relevant chapter and reread the content and you'll soon get back up to speed.

Pace yourself, but keep up the work and it won't be long before a noticeable change starts to take place in you; visible for all to see.

# Chapter 1

# EXCUSES

# About Excuses

**There are many ways of describing what an excuse is, a favourite of mine being: 'a made-up reason for taking no action'. I also like: 'a made-up reason for not accepting responsibility', and 'a made-up reason for defending unproductive behaviour'. Whatever words we use, though, they'll arrive at the same point – a way of avoiding something we don't want to deal with.**

One of the biggest causes of excuses is what I call 'The Big Mountain Syndrome', where you see yourself standing at the base of a mountain, staring up at the summit, and feeling completely overwhelmed – what you want to achieve looks so far away, so hard to reach and requires so much effort that you can't find the energy to even think about conquering the climb. As a consequence, you don't even try.

Sometimes, we make excuses because at some stage in our lives we have experienced a disempowering event that has left an imprint and has caused us to lose confidence. With such experiences in our past we may, consciously or unconsciously, use them as references to affect our current behaviour – so we end up fearing change, fearing making mistakes, fearing embarrassment and looking the fool. We may even exacerbate our lack of confidence by negatively comparing ourselves to others.

Maybe laziness is at work here too, because so many people are looking for 'Easy Street', and this in itself is enough to keep the stream of excuses flowing and keep people right where they are. This is the cop-out route, where we don't actually take responsibility for our choices and related consequences. We find it easier to bury our heads in the sand because change is so hard; we find it too uncomfortable to face big challenges, so we just keep things as they are ... keep things comfortable.

Excuses are often made when what is under consideration just doesn't interest us enough. Maybe a friend has asked us a favour that we think is unreasonable, but rather than risk offending them, we use passive, weak excuses such as "I'm not sure, I'll let you know" rather than unambiguous, strong language that clearly states our position. In this case an assertive "No" would be much easier and would avoid any unnecessary misunderstanding.

Excuse-making is a bad habit that we get into, a bad habit that has consequences which guarantee we will never reach our full potential; it's a form of self-sabotage that will move us away from our goals; we pull the rug from under our feet before we have a chance to step out and make progress; we pull the curtains of possibility before we get a chance to look out and spot opportunities; we devalue our skills and talents before we get a chance to use them.

Really, excuses are a symptom, an effect of negative thinking, leading us in the direction of mental blocks and imaginary walls. They also put us on a tread-wheel, a vicious cycle where they keep us from breaking out of our tight and stifling comfort zones (which could also be called virtual coffins); and this comfort zone trap will manifest more excuses, and in so doing will restrict our creativity and aspirations by giving us a negative focus, pessimistic outlook, limiting beliefs, zero growth and eventually big, big regrets. We could make an excuse to avoid something by saying that we don't have enough time and then justifying that by living a lifestyle that tends to back up and feed this idea. We may subconsciously over-commit by taking on too many responsibilities.

When all is said and done, excuses become obstacles: they stop us moving forward; in a way, they may make us feel safe and guilt-free, tucked away in our cosy little cocoons, unwilling to venture out to enjoy the riches of life for fear of meeting misfortune. Can you imagine what would happen to a butterfly if it decided it was going to stay in its cocoon rather than spreading its wings and flying away?

I believe that one of the best ways of tackling our excuse-making is to create an awareness of when and why we're making them. A little bit of contemplation before implementing the Positive Life-Balance Code into your life can be the first stepping stone to making changes. We can begin by asking ourselves open questions to clarify things.

WHY   *do I keep making excuses?*

WHEN   *do I find myself making them?*

WHAT   *am I missing out on by making them?*

WHERE *can I find a solution?*

WHO   *do I admire, who could act as a mentor and guide me in the right direction?*

HOW   *can I create lasting change?*

Excuse-making is often the difference between people who are going somewhere in their lives and people who are barely moving at all ... and may even be slipping backwards. The more successful someone is, the fewer excuses they make.

The person who's going nowhere and has no plan usually has a whole box of excuses to call on and will often play the blame game to explain away their lack of progress. It's their parents fault, their partner's fault, their boss's fault ... or it's the weather, but never the person in the mirror. They'll tell you why they can't, don't, won't, haven't and aren't, and in doing so they slam the door of opportunity on themselves.

The answer lies in taking responsibility; which in itself can give you confidence in implementing what I call the big 'A' word: Action! By taking action you can propel yourself in the direction of positive change, and with determination you'll gather momentum by sticking to the principles outlined in the PLB Code, and this will surely lead you to a much better place. The day you decide that you're going to change something in your life that you're not happy with is the day when things really begin to change ... in all areas of your life, as it's a knock-on effect. Once you start to see those early tangible successes appear, you'll become unstoppable!

# "Don't make an excuse –make a plan –to make a life."

© 2013 NJT

# The Top Twelve Excuses

During my research for writing this book, I interviewed 100 adults to find out what the top 12 excuses would be when asked the following questions: "Have you or would you consider setting up your own business?" and if the answer was "yes", "Why haven't you done it yet?" The results were as follows:

1. I can't find the time

2. It's too late

3. I don't have the money

4. I don't have the knowledge

5. I don't have the experience

6. I didn't get the right education

7. I don't live in the right town

8. I lack confidence

9. There's too much competition

10. I don't have the contacts

11. I just don't get the breaks

12. I'm too old

Many people will have great ideas for writing a book, building a business ... realising a dream; they'll often talk big and enthusiastically about their project, telling you exactly what they're going to achieve ... and then something happens, maybe fear and/or doubt sneak in through the back door, or other people convince them that their idea is not really that great, but whatever it is, when you catch up with them some weeks or months later, they'll give you every excuse as to why they never got started.

# Meet Excuse-Making Eddie

Excuse-making Eddie briefly thought about the idea of starting a business, but it didn't take long for him to dismiss the 'silly idea' and get back to the real business of watching more TV. When I caught up with him a couple of months after hearing about his plans, it was clear that he hadn't progressed at all. I couldn't help but notice how his excuses rushed like a raging river, gathering momentum, with each one feeding off the previous one and guaranteeing that he stayed right where he was:

**ME:** *"Hey Eddie, I heard you've been thinking about setting up a business?"*

**EDDIE:** *"Yeah ... I was."*

**ME:** *"Why haven't you done it yet?"*

**EDDIE:** *"I'm too busy, I really don't have the time ... anyway, it's too late now – I've missed the top of the market."*

**ME:** *"That's not true, Eddie. Benjamin Franklin said, 'If you want something done, ask a busy person.' Now that's true – busy people are ideal for starting businesses, it's the idle who are not, and there's no reason to believe the market has already peaked."*

**EDDIE:** *"I just don't have the money, the knowledge or the experience."*

**ME:** *"That's not true. You don't need a lot of money to get started; you just need to ... get started. Knowledge can be gained from a plethora of different sources and experience as you go along."*

**EDDIE:** *"I didn't get the right education and I'm not living in the right town."*

**ME:**    *"That's not true; Sir Richard Branson left school at 16 ... and you live close to London!"*

**EDDIE:**    *"If I started this project 10 years ago, I'd be a millionaire by now..."*

**ME:**    *"Very true Eddie, very true."*

**EDDIE:**    *"If only I had the confidence... (long pause). Anyway, there's no point starting now, there's a recession on."*

**ME:**    *"That's not true. You've always seemed such a confident person. Sometimes a recession can be the best time to start a business ... saying that, things are improving now anyway."*

**EDDIE:**    *"There's so much competition out there."*

**ME:**    *"That's not true. There are millions of customers out there; you're creating not competing. You're selling the unique brand of 'you'."*

**EDDIE:**    *"I don't have the contacts."*

**ME:**    *"That's not true; I know a lot of influential people."*

**EDDIE:**    *"I tried it before and it didn't work then – I just don't get the breaks, plus I'm too old now."*

**ME:**    *"That's not true; surely you learnt from your past mistakes? You should be in a stronger position now than you've ever been, and you're only in your mid-forties, you've got plenty of time."*

**EDDIE:**    *"I tend to think success is for other people – it's not for me."*

**ME:**    *"You know what Eddie, I think you're right, it's true – success is for other people, it's not for you ... you were right all along."*

# "An excuse is a 'get-out clause'; the only trouble is some will get you out of a great future."

© 2014 NJT

## A Closer Look At Excuses

Let's randomly select and look more closely at a number of regularly used excuses that, if not addressed, will surely derail our train before we even get started. Some of them are going to have the word 'can't' lurking around. The problem with this word is it gives the impression that something is final and non-negotiable. This little fellow needs to be caught and dealt with. We need to get a scalpel and slice away the 't', thus turning it into something more conducive to creating success: CAN!

### I Can't Find The Time

I remember attending a seminar on creating a positive lifestyle where the speaker, interacting with members of the audience asked a particular individual, "How do you feel about incorporating some physical exercise into your daily routine?" The reply was delivered in a dull monotone, "I would ... but I can't find the time." I must admit I almost groaned out loud. It was without doubt a completely worthless excuse. This person had found the time to come along to the seminar, but couldn't muster up enough energy to do a little exercise at home. If a quality life is important enough to you, believe me, you'll find the time.

# I Can't Do It

Why can't you do it? Have you tried? There's no point saying that you can't play the piano because you're not musical if you've never really attempted it. This excuse will keep you right where you are. It doesn't give you any options for moving forward in life. Giving the impression that you're helpless, powerless and disadvantaged – and we know that's not true. Now, you're going to have to exercise some control here and make some better choices. Develop a measure of fearlessness by focusing on the benefits you'll receive by changing your mindset to one of 'can do'.

# I Can't Change The Past

No, you're absolutely right, but you can learn from it and move on. All of us have some bad memories and some negative conditioning that can come back to haunt us from time to time. Ultimately, the final choice is yours: are you going to choose to move on with your life or to be controlled by past events – events that no longer exist or have any power over you, except the power you give them? Clearly, allowing ourselves to be trapped in some self-created prison cell is not going to help us build an exciting future. It's time to stage a jailbreak and set ourselves free.

# I'm Too Old—It's Too Late Now

I know an intelligent woman who right from her young days would always 'double up' her excuses; for example, when offered job promotions in her twenties to positions she was well capable of excelling in, she would always disqualify herself with a double whammy such as, "I'm too young – I'm not experienced enough." There was always an excuse, and always a follow-up excuse to justify and strengthen the first one. Now, as a more-than-capable person in her forties, who has experienced a lifetime of under-achievement, the double excuses still keep coming: "I can't give up the job I hate – because I've got bills to pay."; "I'm too old – it's too late now."

What age do you have to be to claim your slice of life's cake? Now, if you told me you wanted to be an astronaut and to explore space and you'd just celebrated your 60th birthday, I would probably advise you to focus your attention elsewhere. That's not being negative, that's being real, but as long as your aspirations are in tune with reality, there's not a problem.

"Am I too old to take up weight training at the age of 65?" No, not at all, as long as you take your current age and condition into consideration, and don't try to train as if you were 25, you'll find that weight training will still add significant benefits to your life.

The thing to realise is that so many of the limitations we have are self-imposed, and sometimes they can hinder us by holding us back and depriving us of many of life's richest experiences.

## I Didn't Get The Right Education

It has been proven many, many times over the years that your early education doesn't have to be the be-all and end-all of whether you have a successful life. Without doubt, the deciding factor has to be how you think. If you think that you can be successful, then you can! The bottom line is that life is a continuous learning curve – one long education from beginning to end and the more you engage with it the better.

Of course, being successful in school can be a great foundation for your future, but if for some reason your schooldays were not the most high-flying/highest achieving days of your young life, there are still many ways to redress the balance as an adult. If you have a weakness in writing or mathematics, for example, there's always help at hand in the form of adult education courses, so it's not a case of using a weakness as an excuse for inaction, but instead, asking yourself, "What am I going to do about it?" Just remember, it would be foolish and wrong to allow pride to stand in your way.

# Optimum Balance
## (Creating Balance-Awareness)

Often, when I do seminars and talk to people about going from excuse-making to creating a more resourceful, excuse-free mindset, I like to have a bit of fun with the audience. Firstly, I like to ask the crowd the big question: "Why do we make excuses?" More often than not the answers I get are as we've previously discussed: When we're feeling overwhelmed or lacking in confidence ... a little weak, stressed, lazy ... or when we're just not interested.

For a solution to creating a more resourceful state of mind, I get everyone to stand up, and I say...

"I would like you to think some positive thoughts ... but whilst standing on one leg." Everyone gets to their feet and attempts to follow my instruction. I then say, "So think some positive thoughts ... now if I hurry you up by saying, 'Come on, come on, tell me your positive thoughts,' you may well say, 'Hang on, I need to get my balance first,' and that's the point that I'm making. If you came to me and asked, 'How can I create a happier and more fulfilling life, free of excuses?' I would say, 'Hang on, you need to get your balance first – bring balance-awareness into your life.'"

What am I talking about when I talk of balance-awareness rather than just balance on its own, and why is it so important? Strangely enough, we can never develop complete balance in our lives because there's always something that's going to throw us off balance, so that's why the Positive Life-Balance Code teaches us about creating balance-awareness and it's this that's going to lead us to where we want to go.

My philosophy is based on the fact that there are five main areas – stepping stones if you like – that are all interrelated. All five must be worked on simultaneously, every day, for us to receive maximum benefits. The pay-offs are enormous, with happiness, contentment and fulfilment being top of the list ... and who doesn't want that? That's why it's so important to embrace the excuse-free PLB Code lifestyle with total commitment. It's like riding a bike: to start off with it seems impossible; you wobble from side to side, fall off a few times, get a few cuts and bruises along the way; but once proper balance-awareness is achieved ... you're off – you're flying, you become unstoppable – and then you wonder how you ever found it so difficult to start with.

OK, so bringing balance-awareness into your life is a lot more difficult than riding a bike, agreed, but the principle is very much the same, so why as adults do we struggle to ride the 'bike of life'? I think we've just never made it past the 'wobble stage'; in other words, maybe we need to take some lessons – and that's what this book is all about.

Once you've established the PLB Code lifestyle you no longer have to constantly think about it – it becomes part of life and natural and is just a great way to live.

Introducing it into our lives is the first building block for the foundation that creates that more resourceful state of mind ... free of excuses!

Let's establish what the five life-balance areas are...

# Introducing The PLB Code

The Positive Life-Balance Code (for balance-aware-ness) is a way of living effectively, and choosing to work with it, a lifestyle. Excuse-making is just one of a number of bad habits and problem areas that can benefit from its application.

It's:

■ a recipe with the best ingredients for a healthy life;

■ a road map leading you to a desirable place;

■ a torch – shining light on depression;

■ a foundation stone for positive change;

■ a 'future building' template for children;

■ a survival kit for the unemployed;

■ a blueprint for creating a more resourceful state of mind;

■ a remedy for those suffering from the malady of excuse-making.

The Code is built on the Five-Fitness-Format.

## MENTAL FITNESS: The Control Centre

This area covers how we think – how our minds can be used to accomplish great things or harmful things depending on how we use them. This amazing instrument, more powerful than the world's greatest computers, directs us along the freeway of life, and this journey can be good or bad depending on our mental diet: the 'mind food' we feed in. All of us at one point or another plant the wrong seeds in the gardens of our minds. It's not always our fault but often the result of our upbringing and past conditioning, plus our current environment. Now, our aim is not to apportion blame but to understand ... maybe we had negative parents, unhelpful school teachers; maybe we were bullied at school or just had a lot of defeatist thinkers in our midst, so what do we do now; where do we go from here?

The Code in this area addresses these difficult topics and gives strategies for taking control, living more positively and building confidence. This is achieved by becoming aware of what we say to ourselves – our inner dialogue – and by using positive vocabulary and repetition, giving us a foundation for literally 'changing our minds' and creating a new focus and developing new, bigger goals that empower us to take action. We'll look at changing old habits that no longer serve us, to new habits like assertiveness that help us develop self-respect. Our aim is to understand that 'the engine of desire turns the wheels of success', and if we channel that desire in a productive way, we'll be giving ourselves every opportunity to create a great future, so let's stand up and be counted.

We'll look at our spiritual selves – the mind–body connection – and rid ourselves of 'mind junk': the self-criticism, the criticising of others, the condemning, the complaining and the constant negative focus on everyday trivia – let's turn on the sunshine!

## PHYSICAL FITNESS: The Vehicle

This area is concerned with how we look after our physical bodies. Our bodies are our vehicles for taking us to where we want to go on our journey through life, and all of us, I'm sure, would prefer them to carry us around as effortlessly and as free from pain as possible. It's our vehicle 'of life for life', a vehicle of possibilities, an amazing, complex work of art that should never be neglected – it's all we've got! Give it the respect it deserves!

The Code in this area teaches us how to maximise our physical selves by taking regular exercise, such as playing sports (tennis, badminton etc.), working out with weights, swimming, running ... generally improving our strength and creating greater fitness levels. It covers nutrition – putting the right fuel in the tank. It also considers sexual intimacy, sleep patterns, meditation, massage and our appearance; remember, it's often the case that if you look good, you feel good!

The Code also teaches us to avoid the things that are guaranteed to sabotage our efforts to become more physically vital, such as smoking, excessive alcohol consumption, drug taking, binging on junk foods, not exercising – need I say more?

# RELATIONSHIP FITNESS: Your Connections

This area covers relationships with other people. Whether it's your family, a partner, friends, work colleagues or strangers, unless you've chosen to live your life as a hermit hidden away in some cave out in the wilds, one way or another, you're going to have to deal with other people. Handling all our relationships in honest and open ways is the best way forward; being assertive, and not being afraid to speak our minds.

The Code teaches us the importance of having quality friends, who can significantly enhance our lives. It also gives us guidance on how to handle more difficult situations, such as dealing with 'toxic' people: yes, those serial whiners and complainers who only see the down side of life and unfortunately seem to have an overwhelming desire to dump their negative junk on, or should I say in, your head, at any given opportunity.

We must maintain a positive relationship with ourselves – this can be linked back to the Mental Fitness area and to our self-image. Are we treating ourselves as our own best friend, encouraging ourselves as if our own personal coach, or are we spending way too much time acting as our own critic?

How is our relationship with the environment? Do we treat it as if it doesn't serve any purpose other than as our playground, or are we respecting it and protecting it for future generations?

## FINANCIAL FITNESS: The Oil

This area covers the oil that makes the wheels of our lives turn smoothly – yes, money, and how we earn it, what we do with it and the role it plays in our everyday lives. It's about putting in place the right strategies for attracting money and creating an understanding of how our thinking decides our financial wealth. Our task here will be to examine our mindset to see if we need to make adjustments in order to maximise the chances of money being attracted to us, and once we have it, it staying around. We'll look at how we can plant prosperity seeds in the minds of our children, thus giving them a head start on their journey through life. We'll look at mental blocks that may well be preventing us from living a life of abundance – we may, without realising it, be repelling wealth due to bad habits, and to hanging onto negative beliefs about affluent people and feeling that we're different to them and not worthy of having our own prosperity.

The Code teaches us how to create the right mental attitude towards it and see it for what it is – a form of exchange, a reward for services rendered, oil for the machinery, nothing more nothing less.

## FUN FITNESS: Leisure And Pleasure

This area covers our free time, and taking time out to do the fun things we want to do, for leisure and for pleasure; engaging in the things that we find enjoyable and life-enhancing. These might include: visiting the theatre, the cinema or a comedy club; dancing; taking trips abroad to visit new horizons – trying scuba diving, skiing, swimming with dolphins, etc.; taking cultural trips to expand our understanding of the world we live in ... maybe learn a new language; spending time improving ourselves by joining a Toastmasters club to learn public speaking. Also, taking quality time out for ourselves to just relax and recharge our batteries.

The Code teaches us that inviting fun and laughter into our lives at every opportunity is a healthy and smart way to live.

One of the most noticeable things about the five life-balance areas is that they're all interconnected and inextricably linked. For example, if you decided to have a game of tennis, it would be great for mental fitness, all that brain activity, trying to outsmart your opponent; it would be fantastic for physical fitness, all that running around the court. Plus, if you joined a local club it could be great for meeting new people, and so be positive in the Relationship Fitness area; and, if you were pretty good at it, maybe you could give lessons, making it a winner in the Financial Fitness area. Also, what a fun way of keeping fit!

# "The engine of desire turns the wheels of success."

© 2014 NJT

# The Big D

A great way to begin a life of implementing the PLB Code is to embark on The Big D: The Big Declutter. Clutter around you creates a cluttered mind – it represents chaos and confusion and it lowers your vibration, so this is where we need to take some time to evaluate what we have in our lives and whether it needs to be there ... and then decide what action we're going to take to clean up and clear out the junk. This will help us to see the fresh new path leading ahead of us.

When I talk about junk, I'm not just referring to old clothes that we haven't worn for, say, five or more years, or copious amounts of assorted items in the garage or garden shed; I'm also talking about junk relationships with those people who don't add anything growth-promoting to our lives.

It's best at this time to look at your life as a whole and then select one place to begin; one place for action and then take that first step forward. When was the last time you cleared out your kitchen cupboards and drawers? Maybe this would be a good place to start?

Do you have a collection of supermarket carrier bags for use as waste basket liners or similar? The only problem is that the carrier bags seem to breed and they reproduce at a faster rate than you can use them. How about old butter tubs ... do you have a mini 'leaning tower of Pisa' of 'poor man's Tupperware' using up valuable space in one of your kitchen cupboards? What about an old broken iron or kettle that you kept because "One of these days I'm going to get it repaired!"? The trouble is that day never arrives.

What about the contents of your bedroom drawers and cupboards? Those old scratched sunglasses, for example, that were so fashionable eight years ago, but not anymore. How about those Sunday newspaper magazines that you kept because one or two had a recipe in that you thought you'd like to try one day but you never got round to it? Or maybe there was a special holiday feature in one of them that you wanted to keep, but you can't now remember which one it was in … or even where the holiday destination was, and you haven't really got the time or inclination to go hunting through them to try and find it.

As you sweep through the material things in your life, it would be wise to look closely at some of your relationships as well. If they aren't adding any real value to your short stay on this planet, then maybe it would be wise to also sweep your broom across their path and confine them to history.

Here are the results of my own declutter:

I decided to begin in the bedroom – in my wardrobe. I looked at all my shirts: some were my favourites, the ones that I wore 80% of the time; some were select shirts for specific occasions that I wore 20% of the time, that I still liked; and there were some that I didn't wear at all – they were the ones that were out of fashion, were too old, didn't fit any more, or somehow had gained some hold over me under the banner of sentimental value.

I removed every item from my wardrobe, in turn, for analysis and coupled with a 'take no prisoners' attitude. I made 3 piles.

- Pile 1 – Favourite shirts worn 80% of the time – to keep.

- Pile 2 – Select shirts worn 20% of the time – to keep.

- Pile 3 – Items for charity shops, the bin, recycling or other uses such as cleaning the car.

After finishing with the shirts, I used the same strategy with the rest of my clothes before moving on to other items in the house.

Here is the complete list of all the clutter I removed from drawers, cupboards, wardrobes, the loft, the garage, the garden shed and other places, as part of my preparation for introducing the PLB Code into my life.

- 5 shirts

- 3 pairs of socks

- 1 old pair of shoes

- 1 old suit jacket

- 1 pair of trainers

- 3 old pairs of scratched sunglasses

- 1 old pair of reading glasses with a broken frame

- 1 old toaster

- Some old wall tiles

- 1 out-of-date bottle of cough mixture

- Numerous leaflets about holiday insurance/ home insurance

- 1 old mirror

- 2 paint tins, both with about 1 inch of solidified paint at the bottom

- Various pieces of wood

- Some old bed legs with castors (maybe I'll have a use for them one day ... hmm)

- ...and finally, 2 negative old acquaintances!!

# Now Focus

To achieve success with the Positive Life-Balance Code you need to focus. Don't go at it half-heartedly; give it your full attention, because if you can focus without distraction and exercise determination to make it work for you, then the results will be self-evident. Remember, what you direct your attention towards, you move towards. The more you can home in on the strategies and principles explained here, the more they'll expand in your life, daily, weekly, monthly, yearly. The more laser-like the focus on the benefits that can be gained, the more the negatives will be displaced and any limiting thoughts dispelled and over powered by the new higher-grade thinking.

Use the power of focus like a hand pointing you in the direction of your dreams – let those dreams take root in your spirit. Remember, it's a choice you have whether you focus on possibilities rather than obstacles, seeing your future and your loved ones' futures as bright, with your best years ahead. You can choose whether you see it as being inviting: knowing that whatever happens with the economy, the climate, with population growth etc., if we play our part, act responsibly and respectfully towards the planet and encourage others to do the same, we can all make a difference, both as individuals and as part of the collective human effort, and this will enable us to have peace of mind and flourish. There's nothing to be gained from focusing on and worrying unnecessarily about things that are out of your control. Play your part – and trust the universe.

The more you can hone the skill of focus the more you'll be able to see the pictures in your mind of the life you so often dream of, and the more you do this the stronger this powerful, positive habit will become in your life.

See yourself like the proverbial lion after it has selected its prey: it doesn't think of any other animal that may be around, it doesn't think about the weather, it doesn't suddenly change its mind and start chasing a different target, no, it focuses in on the job in hand and then attacks until the job is complete. Total concentration, no distractions, no doubts and no excuses!

That's the kind of attitude you must adopt when deciding to implement the principles of the PLB Code, so the components work in your life. Ask yourself, "Where is my focus?" Is it directed in a laser-like fashion on the strategies that are going to help you grow as a human being, or are you someone who constantly has their focus directed by other people. They say that you're what you think about all day long ... so make sure that what you're thinking about and focusing on are the positive disciplines that will bring you the results you desire.

# The Importance Of Secrecy

Making a commitment to yourself with regards your personal development is exactly that − a commitment to yourself; it doesn't involve or need to involve anyone else; it's personal! By telling others about your private desires and plans to become more, you open yourself up to other people's opinions and often negative energy. This will cause your personal power to diminish by allowing the ego to become involved. When it comes to something as important as increasing the quality of your brief sojourn on this planet, it's best that we play our cards very close to our chests and maintain a certain degree of secrecy. Otherwise, we may inadvertently invite other people to offer their approval for what we're trying to achieve and if self-development is not their thing, they may well end up convincing you that it's not for you either. As a result, rather than complementing the positives that already exist in your life with the PLB Code, you may instead find all the excitement, hope, energy and promise you had for your future be-coming weakened, as seeds of doubt take root – and all because you didn't trust your own opinion enough. Let's get off to a flying start and decide to keep our plans to ourselves. Remember, everyone else will soon see the amazing improvements taking place ... you won't need to tell them.

## It's time for the solution to excuse-making.

# Ready, get set ... go!

# The Grandmaster and the Student

**THE GRANDMASTE**

*"I must stress the journey that lies ahead of you will be challenging ... there will be roadblocks, diversions, and brick walls that you will need to climb over, go under, go around or smash through. You will be encouraged to step out of your comfort zone and move towards becoming a more active and involved player on life's multifaceted stage of discovery, where the desire for excuse-making is forgotten as courage becomes the norm.*

*You've come here today with a vision and a desire to construct a bright new future, so come out from the shadows and walk towards the light, we are not mushrooms; we do not grow in the dark. With the PLB Code I've laid the foundations and given you the building blocks ... now it's up to you to build your castle. Be bold, be your own best friend, and may your every footstep be divinely guided along the path of greatness..."*

## THE STUDENT

# The Mountain

*You stand at the base of the mountain in quiet contemplation – do you attempt the climb? It will test your resolve to the very limit...*

*You may decide it's too hard, too long ... too risky. You may decide to remain at the base, surrounded by the excuses, the trinkets and the pebbles...*

*"By the wizards of restitution, come join us at the summit, I say, the views are amazing and there's tea ... and diamond-life experiences awaiting you."*

*If you take the easy option, one day Father Time will look you in the eyes and ask, "Why didn't you?" but you won't be able to answer because your voice will be choked into silence and your vision blurred by the tears of forever.*

*I implore you to search the recesses of your soul for those grains of faith, for they are surely there, and then proceed as if your very existence depends on the outcome. You will be walking the steps of a giant ... and the mountain will be yours.*

© 2014 NJT

# Chapter 2

## THE PLB CODE

# MENTAL FITNESS

# What We Allow In (And Keep Out)

**Mental Fitness – The Control Centre – it's all about what we allow in ... and keep out. This can be through our eyes, by what we watch and read; or through our ears, by what we listen to and who we associate with.**

If most of the TV programmes you watch are violent films or negative soap operas, reality shows featuring dysfunctional people or news broadcasts showing rapes, murders and every world disaster in graphic detail, then you're feeding in the wrong stuff ... it's the wrong mental diet! You're feeding in poison for your soul and poison for your spirit ... and it's so easy to do because these are the types of programmes that make up most of the TV that's offered to us ... it surrounds us! Always be on your guard, especially with those mind-numbing reality shows, don't allow the enemy to breach your defences – turn off trash TV before it anaesthetises your mind and your dreams get forgotten. As far as the news is concerned, control how much exposure you have to it. If you catch the news first thing in the morning, there's no need to view it again at lunch time or in the evening, and it's certainly worth being selective to which newspapers you read and avoiding the ones with the often sensationalised and biased content. It's important to be informed about what's going on in the world; it certainly doesn't serve us to be ignorant, but it's better to have a few titbits of the unpleasant rather than to feast on it. When you think about it, our eyes and ears are the principal doorways to our inner world and if we're not selective to what we allow through, we can end up becoming a junkyard full of rubbish that doesn't serve us well – it doesn't build us up, it knocks us down; it doesn't empower us, it weakens us.

Don't try to explain it away with the excuse that it's 'just entertainment'. It's incredibly foolish to allow yourself to be contaminated by these programmes because often they appeal to the base elements of human existence and can very gently nudge you off in a direction in which you had no intention of going. It may seem that no harm is being done, but the damage may well grow invisibly inside until it has no more room, and will then find expression on the outside – showing up in your attitude and your actions. Your life is too valuable, too important and your future is too bright to allow your standards to be lowered and your values challenged by allowing in the wrong content.

It's so much better to treat yourself like a high performance machine where only the best oil is put into the engine. How much better would your system run, how much stronger would you be, how much higher would you fly if you were truly selective over what you invited in? Your mind really is a gateway to the temple!

I remember one time sitting on my lounge floor sorting out some papers; I had the TV on, and suddenly the announcer said it was now time for a particular soap opera where the storylines were always very negative. There was no time for finding the remote control – I threw myself in a corkscrew fashion across the room with my index finger sticking out ready to connect with the off button: I scored a direct hit turning the TV off a nanosecond before the first beat of the theme music. My reaction was – result! It's proof that you can keep the junk out if you're determined.

Another way to keep it out is to anticipate it; see it and reject it in advance. Maybe some of your friends suggest that you go to a social function where you know there are going to be a lot of negative people, people who would love to share their insights and opinions of their favourite reality shows and soap operas with you. You don't have to go! Don't worry about what they think of you; they may think you're dull, boring and anti-social but that's their problem – you know otherwise and you don't need to please them or to explain yourself.

Some years ago a friend of mine took part in an experiment at a university. The first part was to test his reaction to being exposed to messages of despair and graphic images of the darker side of life – he reported that his mood took a nosedive, a downward spiral of negativity ... and it took him over two days to start to recover and climb out of the pit of darkness. A month later he took the opposite test where he was subjected to uplifting messages of hope and success and stunning images of beauty – he reported that he felt high, blissful and amazing and that he saw the world as a place where anything was possible.

Now, these two experiments show the extremes of negative and positive exposure and how it can distort your thinking, but the message is clear, that what we expose ourselves to has an amazing effect in every area of our lives.

I've always liked the various sayings about flying with eagles rather than scratching around with the turkeys. There's nothing wrong with turkeys, but let them hang out with other turkeys, not with you. Keep their thinking habits and action habits outside of you – don't absorb their behaviour – you're not one of them! OK, you can get by scratching and pecking around, but you'll never soar, never reach the great heights of your true potential.

# "Eagles don't need the approval of turkeys to fly high."

© 2014 NJT

Maybe it makes them jealous to see you soaring at a great height while they're pecking around in the dirt; maybe they'd like to soar too but haven't got the discipline to do the work to join you. No discipline, but all the excuses!

# Attitude

Our attitude determines our responses to the experiences we have in life, and those experiences often shape our attitude. It's all about our state of mind, our disposition, our mental view of the world. It can direct us towards a future of achievement and enjoyment, if we keep a balance with which outside influences we allow to enter our world, while staying true to our own mind, morality and beliefs. We can avoid becoming delusional by accepting that realism requires a degree of compromise with the world.

Imagine there's within each of us a dashboard from which our attitude is controlled, with dials to fine-tune our perception of, thoughts about and reactions to all that's around us. Other people may attempt to control the dials, to change our course for the better or worse, but as long as you remember it's you and only you who turns those dials, that it's your choice whether you view life in all its beauty and wonder or in all its misery and gloom. If we're in touch with our inner thoughts and feelings and clear on our purpose in life, then the choice is simple, and there's every reason to expect our attitude to remain positive and upbeat.

When we really think about it, nobody else makes us feel angry or depressed, happy or excited ... it's our own response to the events that come before us that can make us feel a certain way; other people merely put our attitude to the test, but the control is always with us, if we choose to exercise it.

Other people will undoubtedly challenge us and try to assert their influence, sometimes for good, sometimes for bad ... but the final responsibility is always ours. If we want our future to be bright and rewarding, we must defend and protect our attitude with persistence and determination, as in doing so we direct ourselves towards the future that we want rather than that other people want.

Having the right attitude is one of the basic success tools. It must feature strongly in our success philosophy, so having a powerful effect in every area of our lives.

People have often asked me what I would suggest as the number one thing to help them create a bright and cheerful attitude – my answer is always, "Immerse yourself in a positive environment."

# Choices And Decisions

Have you ever been in a situation where you were struggling to make progress in a particular direction, whether professionally or personally, only to see others who, in your eyes have no more talent, ability, money, contacts, etc., than you, making giant steps ahead in that same direction? How are they doing it and you're not?

Maybe they're being decisive and not over-analysing. They're seizing the moment, being proactive, while you're on the side lines waiting for permission. As the old saying goes; "they're jumping off a cliff and building their wings on the way down," while you're waiting for everything to be perfect – which it never will be! You may be allowing fear to show its ugly face, casting shadows of doubt as you contemplate whether your decision is right or wrong; they're more concerned about wasting precious time and opportunities. Life will give us the answers as we move forward rather than if we wait until everything is just right. If we spend too much time studying the layout of the battlefield, which is often called the paralysis of analysis, we will find this to be very detrimental to our positive decision-making.

There's no point getting too caught up in analysing whether every decision we make is the right one ... because we don't know the future. One thing is for sure, though, and that is that the answers will be revealed to us in time as we grow in knowledge, ability, experience and maturity.

So many people get derailed from positive decision-making because they listen to the ego, that feeds on certainty and control and because of this they want to know the path before it's been opened up for them ... they want to know who, what, when, why, where and how everything is going to pan out ... but things never work out exactly as you would like – so stop over-analysing and start trusting yourself and being decisive.

We all have the power to make decisions that can be truly life-changing. We can't necessarily change everything that happens to us but we can change the way we think, feel and respond to all that does happen. Our decisions will shape our destiny.

The best way to get a clear perspective on decision-making is to consider where you are right now and how every decision you've made in the past has brought you to this place; whether you bought a house, got married, moved to a different town, etc., but if there are things about where you are now that you really don't like, then it's up to you to decide what needs changing and then to make some bigger and better decisions to bring about that change. Deciding to incorporate the PLB Code into your life, to move away from excuse-making, could be one of the most important and positive decisions you ever make.

It's time to take an inventory of our lives and make some powerful and clear decisions on where we want to go: where we want to live; our career, our health, our relationships, how we want to spend our time.

Decision-making is a mental process where we as individuals can evaluate available options and hopefully select the one that best suits our needs.

With the decision-making process we need firstly to understand why we need to make the decision. The more clarity we can gain the easier it is for us to decide; we can weigh up the pros and cons and find the best option.

Some decisions have very obvious and easy correct answers, some are made through uncertainty and doubt, some may involve an element of conflict, including confrontations and strong emotions, and others involve an element of risk and outright danger. A good example of the final category is where I've seen footage on the internet of people placing their heads in the mouths of crocodiles and alligators and others wrestling with lions or bears – to me these are prime examples of people making seriously stupid decisions that defy belief.

Often our decision-making reflects what we believe will maximise our gains, health and happiness – and may not always be rationally based.

We should always ask ourselves what feels right when making a decision.

If you're busy pondering over an important one, it's probably best to consult your conscious mind first – how does the problem feel to you in the cold, sober light of day? If you're being logical, which option looks best?

If you're still really unsure ask yourself whether you have a strong feeling one way or the other. Consider both sides of the coin – which feels right? If you have a strong gut feeling, now would be a good time to consult with your unconscious mind, because so often our intuition has an uncanny ability of knowing which decision is right for us – we have to listen beyond the noise and chatter going on in our heads and respect the information that our inner voice is trying to express. Really, our intuition is a decision-making facility that we have to guide us.

# That Gut Feeling
## (My Own Story Of Intuition)

Many years ago I moved to a different town to begin a new life. I needed a job and accepted one through an employment agency. On day one came the realisation that I'd made a big mistake … and no, it wasn't just a case of being negative. I knew it wasn't for me; I had this overwhelming gut feeling. The company had a bad vibe about it. By the end of the second day, I'd had enough. On the third day I turned up just to tie up the loose ends and say goodbye.

A week or so later I received a letter from the managing director expressing his disappointment in the fact that I'd left after 'only two days'. It was signed with an extra-large, arrogant-looking signature (if there's such a thing). I took the letter, got a pair of scissors and cut it up into small pieces over the toilet bowl and then flushed it away. It was a way of removing an unwanted negative from my life.

It turned out that my gut feeling towards the company had been 100% accurate – several months later the company went bankrupt and closed down. Our intuition: it's a powerful thing!

We must be prepared to accept that there will always be some regrets when we make a decision, because if we take a specific road there will always be a different road, with all its own hopes and opportunities that we didn't take. Sometimes we have to pass over something to receive a bigger and better reward, either down the same road or a different one.

# Jack's Story

It was England in the late 1950s and a young Jack was finding his school lessons difficult and uninspiring. He wasn't helped by the fact that he was dyslexic. At this time, little was known about the condition and people who suffered from it were generally treated as if they were stupid, so when the teachers treated him this way … and they being people in authority, he believed them to be right. The result being that at the tender age of 13 he started avoiding school, instead helping out in a local butcher's shop. The other people working there were all considerably older than him, with the next youngest being over double his age. They were impressed with the work ethic of this keen young man and began to reward him not only with money but with cigarettes and alcohol too.

It was this early exposure to drink that was to sow the seeds of future negative consequences. Jack now had a companion that was always there to help ease the pain in times of trouble, to take him to a different place in times of weakness and confusion. A 'bottle of medicine' … that made him feel better when he was feeling bad.

As someone whose nature it was to always do things to excess, the more alcohol he consumed the more he needed and this vicious cycle of destruction was forever expanding in his life. In fact, it became a way of life, often rearing its ugly head in his personal relationships and business affairs with disastrous consequences. In his drunken moments he would unknowingly do stupid things, uncharacteristic things, embarrassing things … and those closest to him, those who loved him the most would find their love pushed to the limits of tolerance. Often it would be the following day's sobriety that would reveal the unpleasant truth of what he'd done the evening before.

Over the years, because of his severe lack of self-belief fuelled by his dyslexia, Jack found it difficult to apply for jobs, feeling that he couldn't be of any value to an employer. He started to do things that felt comfortable, such as working with his hands and using his physical strength. One day he was asked by a friend to help with some building work, which he did, finding that it was something he could do, and do well and that he was more capable than he'd previously thought – before long, he was excelling at it, earning good money and being offered other building jobs ... even having to take on extra hands to cope with the workload. This led to the setting up of his own building business that would survive through nothing more than persistence, determination ... and some trial and error due to his self-confessed naivety and lack of business knowledge. At times it would make good money; other times, whenever alcohol led to him taking his eye off the ball, it would suffer huge losses, not helped by several unscrupulous staff members taking advantage of Jack not always being fully aware of what was going on and extracting money from the company; which on several occasions could easily have led to the company folding. "The truth was that I was using alcohol as an excuse to hide from my feelings of inferiority in communicating with other people; I felt that alcohol gave me my voice."

It wasn't until Jack reached his 50s that the real change came about. He knew that his life had to take a new path but wasn't really sure how to go about it. The answer came when someone he hadn't seen for a number of years came round and commented on how unhappy and edgy he appeared. He offered Jack a glimpse of a new world, by telling him about and then giving him some personal development CDs. These CDs triggered something inside Jack, it was like a light bulb turning on, shedding light on a path that had previously seemed so dark he had doubted it even existed.

He would listen to the CDs over and over again, devouring the content with the same intensity as a dying man quenching his thirst at an oasis in a desert ... he needed this information as much as his next breath; in fact it was his next breath, it was that important to his future. He felt a need to challenge himself, to purchase self-development books and to start actively working at reading, something he'd always avoided because of the mental blocks that his dyslexia had put in place. He also attended some of the top seminars to learn as much as possible about unleashing his true potential. Reading the books made him realise that he had a choice as to how he handled the events in his life: he could take complete responsibility or he could choose to be like a cork bobbing around on the ocean at the mercy of the conditions around him. He was now growing as a person, or to use his own words, "Growing from collapse," – learning from the past to build a structure in his life. He was now making much better decisions...

Another part of his growth stemmed from the clear message from the books and CDs about the importance of good communication, and the recommendation that 'students of success' should join the Toastmasters International organisation to gain as much practice as possible at public speaking, and as a result of following this advice he became much more confident, persuasive and influential in his dealings with other people. This new approach did wonders for his business because he gradually became more able to communicate effectively and to motivate and inspire his staff.

Jack knew that him becoming a better, more confident person wouldn't happen instantly but would be work-in-progress; like the mighty oak, it doesn't appear overnight but grows silently and continuously becoming more of what it is each day.

He knew he had to break the alcohol habit. He would stop for a month before regressing, and then stop for three months, then a year; each time he'd find that as the end of the abstention period came close he'd once again be gasping for his old friend ... the bottle, that had such a hold it would always win through. That was when he decided that if he declared that he was going to stop forever, there would be no intense period of longing towards the end of the abstention period because there would be no end to the abstinence. It was in this moment of decision that the new path really opened up in front of him.

In my interview with Jack it became clear that he was operating from a position of bad decision-making, a path of negativity and weakness that stemmed from a feeling of inferiority from his schooling that was re-inforced by his teachers who had no understanding of his dyslexia. However, after studying personal development and implementing the PLB Code over the last two years, he has a completely revised his opinion of himself and operates from an excuse-free position of strength.

## Jack's old negative path of poor decision-making:

He felt stupid when he was at school because of his dyslexia and the way the teachers treated him, and decided to stay away from learning. He decided that he needed alcohol to 'give him his voice', but consumed it to excess. He decided that he was inferior and couldn't be of any value to an employer and so would never amount to much in life; choosing to be a friendless victim and refusing to take responsibility for himself.

## Jack's new positive path of powerful decision-making (following the PLB Code):

Accepting the fact that his dyslexia made his schooldays difficult, but now that he has a better understanding of the condition, he knows it certainly doesn't make him stupid. He actively works on his reading and writing as much as possible, knowing that these will never be his strengths but can be significantly improved with consistent effort on his part.

Deciding to refuse to blame his former teachers for the way they treated him, acknowledging the fact that they were operating from a position of lack of understanding rather than any personal agenda.

Actively deciding to join Toastmasters International to practise communication at every opportunity; and this coupled with the decision to remove alcohol from his life permanently would enable him to 'find his voice' naturally in a supportive environment of learning which would lead to fresh opportunities and many new friends.

Deciding to take responsibility for himself and, in so doing, create his own magic in life without the help or need of alcohol.

# Habits

What is a habit? A habit is the end result of a thought or action which has been repeated until it has become an automatic. Both good and bad habits are learnt and reinforced with repetition. Creating new, empowering ones in place of the self-destructive ones you may already have can take discipline and effort.

Your bad habits can hinder your progress through life more than you think because once a habit has become entrenched, you become its slave. Do you habitually talk negatively about yourself and/or others? Do you habitually see the down side of every situation that comes your way? Is your mind full of fear and apprehension about the future? Do you need cigarettes and alcohol to help dissipate stress? Gaining awareness and understanding that these negative habits have been learnt gives you the ability to replace them with positive alternatives.

It has been stated that the human brain takes around twenty-one days to create the first strand of a new neurological pathway (the beginning of a new habit pattern being formed in the brain). This is the first step towards a new habit, but only the first step; it takes at least two years of constantly reinforcing the new pattern before it becomes a permanent part of you.

It's important to recognise that bad habits are just that – bad habits. If you think back to when you were a child, you never went around craving cigarettes or alcohol or criticising yourself or others, so it's clear they're things we have learnt; which means the next step is to replace them with something better, for they're our enemies and we need to make a decision to exercise control over them and not let them control us. You're in the driving seat and you need to do the driving, starting now!

It's very helpful to see yourself in your mind's eye as the kind of person who you plan to be once you've 'busted that bad habit'. If you've been a smoker, think for a moment about someone offering you a cigarette and how totally in control you'll feel when you say, "No thanks, I don't smoke!" Picture in bright, vivid detail a fitter, healthier you, and make it your practice to run this positive mental movie through your mind, not just once but time and time again. Just keep doing it!

Contemplate the reasons why you want to change a certain habit. Maybe your long-term goal is to make yourself more attractive, to be generally fitter and happier.

It can sometimes be beneficial to start off small, but just as committed, with your steps to busting bad habits. You could do your shopping in a different store on a different day, take a different route to work, rearrange some of your furniture – anything to remove some of the sameness from your life ... and never lose sight of the you who you really want to be.

Use habit-busting as an essential tool for a new beginning. It's time to realise that you're so much more than you have allowed yourself to be in the past – bad habits such as looking back at past failures and using them as an excuse not to move forward encourage only stagnation. Who you were five or ten years ago is not who you are or have to be now; the world has changed and so have you. It's time to show what you're made of. Imagine a teacher writing on your school report, "Always shows great determination"; "Doesn't know the meaning of the word 'defeat'"; "Always displays incredible perseverance and a winning attitude". Well, as an adult, it's time for you to write your own school report and to become a 'professor of purpose'. Show some determination and resilience, because often the person who succeeds is the one who's still working when the masses have all packed up and gone home.

# The Convenience Store

Many years ago I was working in retail and I'd developed a particular bad habit. Next door to where I worked there was a convenience store where I'd go at lunch time and buy my fill of junk food – every day without fail! There was an assortment of confectionery, a bottle of a certain world famous fizzy drink and one or more bags of crisps.

This was a bad habit I needed to bust! I looked on it as a challenge and I thought of ways to make myself accountable by giving myself an extra incentive. I made a decision to not go into that shop again for one year. I then openly declared my intention to a work colleague and told him that if I did go into that particular shop and buy any junk food in the next twelve months, I would give him £50. His face lit up as if he thought "Easy £50 coming up here". Unfortunately for him, he didn't realise how strong my resolve was; he never did receive £50 as I didn't visit that shop at all during the next twelve months.

# Positive Self-Talk

There's always something going on in our minds: a continuous flow of internal dialogue and images – this is the process of thought. It's like our own personal 'mind-theatre' and everybody's is different, so is the 'show' that's being put on by your mind positive? Is the constant chattering by your inner voice supporting you, showing you pictures that excite you; does it constantly remind you of how special and unique you are? It's great when your inner voice is like a coach, encouraging you, boosting you up, motivating you and building your confidence; but it's not so good when it's like an inner critic, continuously undermining you, criticising you, knocking you over and then kicking you when you're down.

The reality is that your mind has become conditioned by repetition, the script that it's working to has been moulded and shaped by the various goings on in your environment over many years. It's important that we understand through awareness what it's saying; when it's being less than encouraging, and then to take control and change it. We really do need to catch it and correct it.

I don't for one minute expect everyone to be thinking positively all the time, in fact I don't think it would be possible – we all get negative thoughts rearing their ugly heads quite often, but it's whether we allow them to take hold or practise swapping them for something more empowering that counts.

We're the pilots of our lives and it's up to us to lead and not be led, to specify clearly what we want and not be controlled by an inner voice that may just be relaying long-term absorbed negativity. Part of the process of making our self-talk positive involves changing our environment and mixing with people who nourish us in every way.

We all know the effects of negative self-talk can bring us to our knees. It can sap our energy, kill our enthusiasm, induce illness, take away hope and leave our personal power so weakened that we may question whether it still exists; and if it's left to continue wreaking its havoc we become completely cut off from our power source – as with a house full of electrical appliances, we're lifeless and unable to function until the power is switched on.

The following are examples of self-talk that leave us totally disempowered.

- ■ "I can't..."

- ■ "I'm no good at..."

- ■ "Everybody's got it in for me..."

- ■ "I don't know how to..."

- ■ "It's hopeless..."

- ■ "I know I'm going to fail..."

This is the kind of self-talk that locks you into a self-created straitjacket. It will, if left too long, guarantee you defeat. It will condition your mind to accept failure before you've even attempted a particular task, a task that with a different mental approach could without doubt be accomplished by you with ease. We need to eradicate these verbal enemies now.

Let's look at:

- ■ "I'll try to ... but;"

- ■ "I really should ... but;"

- ■ "I wish I could ... but;"

- ■ "I ought to ... but."

Unfortunately, these all have an insidious three-letter word – 'but' that's followed by an excuse. "I'll try to get a better job ... but I don't feel that I'm smart enough."; "I really should exercise more ... but I don't really have the time."; "I wish I could improve my tennis ... but I'm not very good at sports."; "I really ought to take a holiday ... but I'm not sure if I can afford it." The sad thing here is you already know where you're going wrong but for whatever reason are choosing to do nothing about the situation. Nothing will change until you do!

Positive self-talk, on the other hand, lifts us up; it adds fuel to the fire of enthusiasm: our psychological ignition system. My own favourite saying is: "It puts fire in your belly and steam in your veins!"

Those with mastery of the positive are always so popular, they're people magnets; others are drawn to them like moths to a light, because let's face it, we all like being around people who build us up, people who give us hope, who demand victory, not defeat, who, when faced with a problem automatically focus on solutions, people who when there's no path, forge their own. We all know that these are the people who are truly connected to the source. It's as if they're party to some universal secret that the majority has not been told about ... or maybe they're just living smart, living intelligently by studying the PLB Code. That 'secret' is here for all to discover!

The people who take the time to study the Code often develop a 'can do' attitude; they become solution rather than problem-oriented. They take the time to show gratitude and affirm the good that's in their lives and these positive statements leave all doors open for them. They repeat, repeat and repeat positive words and statements to instill an expectation of success, now and in the future. They're affirming that they're in the game and mean business, a participator rather than a spectator. These words are the seeds that grow success in their lives ... it's a natural law that cannot err, that you get what you plant ... if you plant tomatoes, you get tomatoes, if you plant nettles you get nettles, so if you plant thoughts that use positive words as building blocks in your subconscious, words that are uplifting, encouraging and inspiring ... then future success is almost guaranteed.

# "Positive self-talk: it puts fire in your belly and steam in your veins."

© 1986 NJT

## Positive Vocabulary

Can positive vocabulary really make a difference to your life? I believe it can make a massive difference, because of the effect it has on your mood. If somebody asks you how you're feeling and you reply dejectedly: "Can't complain."; "Not bad considering."; or "Bearing up under the strain." you're not going to feel very alive or inspired ... and nor is anyone else!

If somebody asks you how you're feeling and you reply with emotional force, "Unstoppable!"; "Fired up!"; "Inspired!" Then not only will you feel one hell of a lot better, you'll also put smiles on the faces of the people you're talking to, as your enthusiasm shines through. There have been times in the past where I had a little fun with some people (admittedly who I knew quite well) – when they asked me how I was feeling, I'd reply loudly, "Cosmically energised!" On another occasion, I would say, "Wired to the mains!" Complete with some relevant gestures thrown in for good measure. It never failed to raise a smile to the extent that they would look forward to when they saw me again, just so they could hear my latest mantra. Now, I don't think this would be appropriate if you were, for example, meeting with some business associates with the aim of making a sale ... it might actually lose you the deal. Cautious enthusiasm would probably give you more chance of making your pitch successful.

How does positive vocabulary work? It's simple! As children we learnt the meaning of words. If, for example, I asked you to think of the word 'happiness', you would instantly think of all the meanings you were taught that you associate with this word, such as smiles, laughter, sunshine, parties, optimism. If I asked you to think of the word 'depression', once again you would think of all the associated meanings you were taught, such as greyness, dullness, helplessness, illness, pessimism. It's all to do with where you put your word association focus. The word 'happiness' can trigger the feel-good factor with positive effects on your mood. Alternatively, the words associated with 'depression' can send you into a negative downward spiral, unless you take control of your thoughts and your focus and redirect them.

I once worked with a woman, who when asked how she was feeling at the beginning of the week, would often reply, "Mondayish," I thought this was a very disempowering and pessimistic response as it was delivered with a negative and defeatist inflection. What she was really saying was: "It's the first of five days of drudgery, the weekend seems like miles away and I don't really want to be here, so I'm giving myself permission to be unhappy." I tried to explain that Monday was no different to any other day and that each day carried with it its equal quota of pleasures and opportunities. What she was effectively doing was writing off all the weekdays and only giving herself permission to be happy at weekends, but with that kind of negative attitude, when the weekend finally did come around, she would probably make herself unhappy because it was raining or cold.

I remember in the mid-1990s, I enrolled on a computer course where one of the tutors was a gentleman named Colin – a little grey-haired man around 60 years of age. Now Colin had a great way with words. If you took an exam and you failed, he'd write on your paper "Not yet achieved." I thought this was a particularly good use of words. Instead of the person who hadn't passed going away feeling like a failure, they would now go away feeling disappointed but in the knowledge that they would more than likely pass next time ... and all because of Colin's clever and kind use of words.

# "Let's colour up our lives and paint our own rainbows."

© 2003 NJT

Every time you use positive words and expressions, you're allowing psychological sunshine to enter your world. You know how you feel in winter when there has been a succession of dull, cloudy days, your mood starts to get a little dull and cloudy too, but once the sun shows its warm face and showers you with its glorious light, your mood lifts and you feel alive and energised. This is the effect you have on yourself and others when you use words that inspire and excite ... they change us for the better, so let's colour up our lives and paint our own rainbows as we affect positively those around us. Often our words are like verbal boomerangs – what we throw out there, is what we tend to get back, so let's use words that are like verbal vitamin pills rather than cyanide capsules. Let's spread the good news!

# "Our words are like verbal boomerangs – what we throw out there, is what we tend to get back."

© 2003 NJT

## Being Positive To Others
(What You Give Out You Get Back ... Usually!)

In my younger days I took up a position as a trainee manager at a well-known holiday park by the sea.

I didn't know anybody at this place and wondered what the best way of making new friends was, so that my stay would be as enjoyable and positive as possible.

Getting to know people was actually very easy because everyone was required to wear a name badge, and so, I decided from day one that I would be upbeat and enthusiastic with everyone I came into contact with, regardless of which department they worked in, as on the whole, people like to talk to positive people and to hear their names being used – is there anything sweeter than the sound of your own name? This is because on a subconscious level we crave recognition and to be treated as if we're individuals and matter. My strategy wasn't about being manipulative though, but about being friendly.

There was a memorable occasion when I met up with two work colleagues to go for a drink about three weeks after starting. Our route from the staff block meant that we had to walk across the park to get to the bars. As we walked along a man in a grey suit walked past. "Hi Neil," he said smiling. "Hi Dave," I replied. As we carried on a large man in a uniform crossed our path. "How are you doing Neil?" "Pretty good, thanks Steve." Two young girls walked by. "Hi there Neil." "Hi girls." Then a young lad with a baseball cap. "Alright Neil?" "Yeah... and you Craig?" and finally a very scruffy individual. "Off to the bars then Neil?" "That's right Sean!"

One of my colleagues looked at me stunned and said, "Who are they?" and the other said, "How do you know all them?"

"The guy in the grey suit is the manager of the accounts department, the big guy is a security guard, the two girls are cleaners, the young guy with the baseball cap runs the go-karts and the scruffy guy scrapes the plates after you've had your dinner in the staff canteen ... I know them because they all wear name badges ... and I talk to them!"

On another occasion I went to the staff canteen with the same two colleagues. I knew that on this occasion what was on the menu was not very appetising. My colleagues in front of me made their selections; suddenly, the person serving the food said, "Here you go Neil, I saved you this," and passed me a massive jacket potato. "Thanks Frank." I headed towards the table where the other guys were going. They hadn't noticed what I had on my plate. Suddenly there was a chorus of "Where did you get that?" "The guy behind the food counter is called Frank, he's got a name badge and I talk to him." What you give out, you get back!

Another example was when I tried to get a staff parking permit, but if you were a trainee this proved impossible, which meant that you had to find a parking space down a side road as you weren't allowed to bring your vehicle onto the park itself. Parking down the side roads was a lottery, as young people frequenting the local bars and clubs would pass by them and often do damage while in a state of mild inebriation – it wasn't uncommon to find a hub cap missing or a windscreen wiper ripped off. For me, it was a hub cap. I expressed my concerns to my security guard friend who suggested I bring my car round to the back of the complex, where he would reserve a space for me very close to the security post, and would give me a cone to put in front of the space when I went out so it was reserved for me for when I got back. What you give out can sure reap rewards if you're friendly and positive!!

During my time working at the park, I had a proud boast: I could go into the staff canteen for dinner and guarantee that I could find a space at a table to sit with people I knew ... every time!! The tables seated four and there was always one with a space for me, whether it was with the receptionists, security guards, cleaners etc. That was until a day arrived when many of the regular staff had left and a lot of new staff were starting. I stood in the queue and panned across the hall; there were no spaces with people I knew ... except one ... opposite Big John. Big John worked in the stores, and he had a problem; an unfortunate habit, and he would share his problem habit with you. If you engaged him in conversation he would share his saliva with you. He wasn't malicious, it was just his problem, so having a conversation with him was a bit like standing on the sea front with waves crashing against the rocks ... you tended to get sprayed! Sit opposite Big John or sit with strangers? That was the choice I had to make ... after thinking briefly about my meal and what was likely to happen to it if I sat opposite him, I wandered down the aisle with my tray and joined a table with three young guys. I introduced myself, read their name badges and made three new friends. My focus switched to the meal in front of me. Suddenly, I heard an angry voice from the front of the room shout, "Stop spitting on my dinner!" I glanced round and smiled. Sometimes you just know you've made the right decision.

My point here is that generally what we give out we get back, whether that's negative or positive ... although what Big John was giving out was probably an exception to the rule.

# Self-Esteem

A little over two years ago, Dave and Steve, who had never met, shared a common desire. They'd both spent many years working for other people and had now reached an age where the thought of setting up a business and working for themselves was becoming very appealing. Due to past set-backs and disappointments Steve had developed an extremely negative attitude towards people, the economy, the government, the weather ... in fact, life in general. Dave, on the other hand, felt optimistic and actively sought out new ways of building his confidence, and in doing so discovered the Positive Life-Balance Code and decided to use it as part of his tool kit towards helping him create a successful business venture.

Here we are two years down the road and Dave seems to be making great progress. He and others have noticed a remarkable change taking place. His levels of confidence seem to have risen sky-high, he has more poise and his speech seems more fluent with his words being delivered with greater clarity and conviction.

Steve, on the other hand, started off half-heartedly, never fully committing, never fully believing ... he doesn't expect much for his efforts ... it all seems too much like hard work. It's not long before he's ready to quit, exclaiming that he doesn't get the breaks, so what's the difference between Dave and Steve? Self-esteem! That is, confidence in one's own worth and abilities.

It all boils down to the fact that Dave decided to make a bigger and better decision than Steve; he chose to commit to improving his self-esteem through the PLB Code

... and it's the commitment that made the difference. Basically, Dave was focusing on where he was going to and Steve was focusing on what he was going through. The result being that Dave started experiencing tangible success almost immediately, with his self-esteem increasing every day, while Steve barely got started; in fact, essentially he stayed right where he was and sometimes even slipped backwards. His low self-esteem was noticeable by his poor posture and in the fact that he was becoming more and more critical of himself and others. His focus was always on the dirty ground, never the blue sky, always on darkness, never on the light, always problems, never solutions, always excuses, never action. Sometimes life seems almost too much trouble for him – he's easily discouraged, often depressed, feels isolated, unloved and bored. He gets angry easily and becomes overly pre-occupied with everyday trivia. "I just feel that life is passing me by," is one of his frequent laments; "I feel like a party balloon floating on a breeze with no idea where I'm going," is another.

Self-esteem is about how you see yourself. It's such an important part of your self-concept, that a lack of it can seriously hinder your development as a human being, with serious implications as far as your relationships with other people are concerned, and can also affect your future career prospects.

An important thing to realise about this learnt hopelessness and helplessness is that you're not as trapped as you may think you are. Changing things for the better may not be that difficult, as Dave has proven by putting into practice the ideas presented in the PLB Code and by using it as a foundation to improve focus and replace bad habits with more productive ones.

He enjoys being on the upward spiral, and freely admits that he feels much more outgoing, finds it easier to express himself, and feels confident about reaching his goals and this is reflected in the way he moves; his energy and purpose. 'Seize the day' is his often-heard battle-cry. He's optimistic, free from anxiety, radiates an inner calm and can be terribly irritating with his constant cheerfulness. People often comment on how self-assured he appears.

# "The higher your self-esteem the easier it is to handle adversity."

© 2013 NJT

Without doubt, Dave's ever-rocketing self-esteem doesn't allow him to just dabble with success – he now expects it. This positive attitude propels him forward to make his business goals a reality. Steve, however, is unfortunately just so unconvinced that he can achieve his goals that he goes about his tasks somewhat half-heartedly with a subconscious expectation of failure, and so it becomes his reality – a self-fulfilling prophecy. This negative downward spiral he finds himself caught up in can only be reversed by following the PLB Code with 100% commitment – as Dave has done. Remember, half-heartedness will get you half-hearted results!

Research shows us that people who feel good about themselves tend to pay more attention to other positive information about themselves, while those who feel bad pay more attention to other negative information about themselves. You know how it is, once you start rolling in a particular direction, it can be very difficult to apply the brakes, stop and change direction. Once your self-esteem has found its level – you tend to bias incoming information. A person with high self-esteem will ex-

plain away a failure and build on their already significant successes while a person with low self-esteem will
explain away a success and spend the rest of their time
running away from failures.

Let's not mess around, self-esteem is serious stuff! By
working on yours daily you can use Dave's example to
soar to new heights – with results coming remarkably
quickly. All it takes is commitment, and an investment
of time. Are you ready to take possession of your future?

Two ways in which we can initiate a revolution for our
self-esteem are contained in the PLB Code:

The first is to review our thinking habits and the subsequent results which are showing up in our lives (cognitive). The second is to actively work on the strategies for
positive change (behavioural).

# Self-Image

Let's take a look at something that can be the deciding
factor in determining exactly how successful we are and
how successful we're likely to become – our self-image. This is most definitely where the foundation of our
success is built. Self-image is how you see yourself. In
other words, if you're feeling really happy about and accepting of yourself, you find it so much easier to express
yourself clearly and concisely and say what you really
feel. It's a fact that if you love being who you are, the
world can seem like a better place and you're more likely to have positive thoughts and also more likely to mix
socially, and it then becomes a positive loop; you get
back what you give out. Every thought you have directs
your behaviour within the confines of your self-image,
whether positive or negative. This inner picture of you
has been gradually built up over many, many years by
events that have happened and experiences you have
had which have shaped your beliefs. Consequently, you

end up living your life within the parameters of this image. It's built on:

- How you rate your looks;

- How attractive or not you feel your personality is;

- The kind of person you believe yourself to be;

- How you think others see you;

- What you think others think of you;

- How much you like yourself;

- How much you think others like you;

- Your success levels and your status.

As a result our self-image will determine:

- How successful we are at forming meaningful relationships;

- How much success we achieve in our careers;

- How much happiness we experience;

- Whether we live a life of open accomplishment or just a pinched existence.

If you want to revolutionise your self-image then now could be the time to try out some new disciplines to kick-start the process. You may feel awkward when you first start experimenting with new behaviours – but just you check out the results! You'll be astounded!! The day you make friends with yourself and decide that you're worthy of fair, respectful treatment at all times from friends, family and workmates, and will accept nothing less, is when your life will improve beyond recognition. When you openly declare your value, people will respond.

Let's face it, we're all part of the universe – nobody is more or less worthy of a good life than anyone else. Although some people may be worthy of more respect than others, by the way they behave: holding themselves to a higher standard, and others because they've made greater sacrifices to become competent in certain professions, such as a doctor, a surgeon, a pilot or a scientist or they've achieved major success in sport, art, business or in some philanthropic way. Whatever you become in life, though, your right to take your seat in the theatre of humanity doesn't change whether you're the Queen of England, a famous rock star, a road sweeper or a window cleaner – the important thing is we are all equal. Your status, your looks, your salary – none of these determine your worth. Your worth as a human being is the same as anyone else's and as soon as you realise this simple truth and take it on board the better ... it's never positive to raise someone else's head above your own.

It's a shame that so many people remain trapped in the self-made prison cell of poor self-image. Some people may argue that all the negative experiences they've had over their lifetime have 'sentenced them' to a life of mediocrity and drudgery and there's nothing they can do about it. The real truth is that you're always in possession of the golden key that unlocks the door to freedom. You carry this key around with you all the time – it's in your mind: you may unfortunately have been conditioned not to see it, but this doesn't mean that it's not there. By making a small adjustment in your focus you may find that not only do you have access to the key, but with a different perspective, you may realise that your prison cell has paper-thin walls anyway, so breaking out may be easier than you think.

Our self-image is like a computer program; basically it gives us back what we put in. What is allowed into the subconscious will take root there; so, if over the years negative seeds have been allowed to grow, then they're going to produce more of their own. If you've been led to feel bad about yourself you can actually induce illness or manifest accidents. These could be seen as subconscious punishments metered out to hurt you when you don't like yourself.

By reinforcing a bad self-image you may actually find yourself sabotaging your own happiness. When an opportunity comes along you may find many reasons or excuses why you can't seize it, so you end up missing out, or not even attempting.

Some people with a distorted self-image have, for many different reasons become quite obsessed about a specific part of their body that they've been led to believe was unattractive:

## Emma's Story

**I was once introduced to a beautiful 16-year-old girl called Emma, who had become incredibly self-conscious about her nose. I'd actually been told about this before I met her, but it was clear from her body language that, to her, her nose stuck out about three feet and was about one foot wide. All the time she was talking to me, she was constantly putting her hand across her face, in a vain attempt to hide this awful appendage. This kind of behaviour, if anything, made you look at her nose even more, but the saddest thing of all was that as far as I could see, it seemed perfectly normal – in fact it was quite attractive.**

It turned out that, when she was growing up, Emma's somewhat ignorant and insensitive father had often called her 'big nose' as a put-down. I'm sure he must have found some warped humour in this, but poor Emma, being young and impressionable and susceptible to the power of suggestion, took it to heart and developed a 'negative focus' every time she looked in the mirror. The result being that, with her distorted beliefs, whenever she saw her reflection she saw this face with a giant nose staring back at her ... and the power of this belief, being so strong, eliminated any positives, such as the fact that she was very pretty, had lovely hair, a beautiful complexion, great teeth, etc.

# What do you see when you look in the mirror?

If you see yourself as being no good at something and you keep repeating this negative message to yourself, then eventually, with enough reinforcement your sub-conscious mind will accept it as true. Say, for example, you once had a bad experience in the classroom. You entered an exam and you came bottom, and now you tell yourself and anyone else who'll listen that you were never any good at mathematics or English or whatever the subject may have been, with the result being that you don't even try anymore and it becomes a self-fulfill-ing prophecy. The more these negative messages are re-peated the more firmly they become embedded in your self-image. The good news is if it works so well with the negative, it's going to work just as well with the positive.

We need to start seeing ourselves in a bright new light. If you're unhappy when you look in the mirror, maybe it's time to remind yourself of your good points.

I believe there are ten steps of awareness we can use to improve our self-image:

# Step 1: Self-Acceptance

If, for example, there's a specific part of your body that you're very unhappy with ... you have a choice: you can decide to accept it and not allow your dislike to grow out of all proportion, especially if it's something you can't change, like your height or bone structure; or you can make your life a misery by constantly focusing on it negatively. If it's something minor that's making you unhappy, such as an unsightly birthmark, or an old tat-too that was great when you were young but you've now out-grown it, then find out whether you can get it fixed. If you can, that's great! Spend the money and look at it as an investment in you and your future ... but if you can't, then we must concentrate once again on accept-ance and not allow ourselves to focus on it in a negative way, robbing ourselves of present-moment joy.

Point of resistance: When you're looking in the mirror and you're about to think those habitual disempowering thoughts ... Stop! Focus on your many good points.

## Step 2: Compliments

It's clear that our self-image determines how we think about things ... it directs our focus; if our self-image is really positive, it becomes very easy to accept compliments from other people.

Notice when you receive a compliment how good it makes you feel ... and the person giving it. It's a gift from one person to another. How about making a complimentary gift to yourself? When was the last time you paid yourself a compliment?

Learning self-love doesn't have to be seen as fuel for making us big-headed and conceited, but by having a healthy self-respect we can receive compliments for what they are – and not deflect them as if they're undeserved.

A healthy, mature way to handle a compliment is to accept it with a simple "Thank you." There's no need to feel awkward or embarrassed and to start trying to explain away success. If, for example, someone commented on the fact that you made a really great presentation today, don't reply by saying, "Well, it could have been better," and then start pointing out all the bad points that you weren't happy with. A compliment is a gift that should not be thrown back at the person giving it.

Point of resistance: The moment when you've been given a compliment and you're about to throw it back ... Stop! Just say "Thank you."

## Step 3: Build Yourself Up

Be your own champion; be your own superstar – give yourself a pat on the back when you do something well. It's customary for us to do the opposite, to berate ourselves when we make the smallest mistake, but let us today make a small change in our thinking and start to act a little smarter, and shower ourselves with compliments and warm praise for all the good things we've done. Every one of us has things that we should be proud of, so let us take a few moments to remember them and congratulate ourselves. Never miss an opportunity to build yourself up by acknowledging these accomplishments, however small they may be, and while there's nothing wrong with admiring someone else who has achieved something great, never put them on a pedestal as if they're a superior being.

Many years ago I met a man who delighted in showing me pictures of his 14-year-old son pictured individually with all the players from a world famous football club. One thing that was very noticeable when looking at these photos was that he (the father) seemed a lot happier about it than his son was ... who looked quite miserable in every picture! It was quite clear it was the father who was the real 'hero-worshipper', who revealed his feelings of being unworthy by getting a pair of registration plates for his car with one of the footballers' names on them.

I actually asked him if he thought teaching his son hero worship was a good idea and wouldn't it be better to teach him to admire and respect his own abilities, because you can be sure that his son was better at certain things than were some of these 'superhumans' he was being taught to look up to ... maybe he could write better than them, do maths better than them, sing better than them, who knows?

Many people admired and hero-worshipped Elvis Presley – and still do now, many years after his passing. I admired the fact that he was a great singer and a charismatic performer, and unique (just like we all are), but often when you're offering up great admiration, it's to your perception of the person, a public persona, an image rather than reality. The 'King of Rock 'n' Roll', the money, the girls ... if you'd actually known him you may have found him to be quite an ordinary guy. Maybe Elvis didn't really like Elvis, because he knew he wasn't the amazing person the public thought he was; maybe at the time of his demise he was getting a little tired of being sold as something that challenged his authenticity – maybe he just wanted to be 'normal', with a loving relationship rather than being too famous to go anywhere.

It's so important that we spend our time being our own hero and liking ourselves, because if we live to be a ripe old age we're going to be spending a lot of time with ourselves and who wants to spend a lifetime with someone they don't like?

Point of resistance: Whenever you're about to partake in a self-putdown ... Stop! Switch to a powerful, positive self-build-up.

## Step 4: Your Behaviour Is Not Who You Are

Don't let a silly mistake affect your self-image by making you feel like a fool – a mistake is proof that you were trying to accomplish something ... you may not have got it right but if it's used as a learning guidepost then it would be wise to see mistakes as valuable, so that we get it right next time. Mistakes are OK, they're allowed, they help us grow and by accepting them we allow ourselves to keep our self-respect.

I remember some years ago I was visiting a quiet part of the United States; I'd driven over a causeway that went for a couple of miles to an off-shore island. After spending the day exploring I was ready to head back to the city. There were no other vehicles around when I got back to the causeway. As I drove on, being in America, I started to drive down the right-hand side; after about a mile I happened to glance in my rear-view mirror and noticed several cars some way behind were driving on the left. I looked up and there was a sign: it said, "DON'T DRIVE ON THE HARD SHOULDER"... that was me, I put my hand up, I made a mistake, it doesn't define who I am ... it was just a mistake and we all make them. Another time, I drove into a car park and there was a car coming towards me; "get over, you idiot" I gestured. The other car driver duly obliged only to reveal the white arrows pointing to me; yes, I'd driven in the exit, I made a mistake and it doesn't define who I am. You may be thinking, "This guy must have been a complete nightmare when he was in the States." No, I was driving around for three weeks and only made two mistakes. What about all the times I got it right? Why do we always remember the mistakes?

Point of resistance: When you're about to berate yourself for doing something stupid ... Stop! Remind yourself of all the great things you've done.

# Step 5: Make Sure Everybody Knows How You Are To Be Treated

Strangely enough, we can gauge our self-image by monitoring how people around us behave towards us. People who have a healthy self-image behave in an 'I respect myself' way, and by doing this they're effectively laying down rules of 'expectation of treatment' – they send out subtle messages to people, saying here is an important person who should be treated with respect.

There are subtle messages or 'tells' in the way you walk and talk and in the way you present yourself that silently broadcast to other people how you expect to be treated. You need to manage what you're subconsciously putting out there in order to maximise a positive response from others.

If you find that you're being treated, let's say, less than respectfully, at any time, then maybe you're giving the impression that you don't matter that much and aren't very important ... maybe you feel your opinion doesn't matter or wouldn't be listened to. All this is doing is weakening your personal power.

What 'giveaways' are there here? What 'tells' are there? Are you displaying poor posture – with meek and passive body language? Is your voice quiet and sounding as if you don't believe the words you're saying? Are your body movements hesitant and indecisive? All these components added together create a very negative, submissive and subservient picture in the minds of observers, so what do they do? They treat you in accordance with the image you're projecting. They're responding to the pictures you're painting. If you've painted a picture in their minds of you as a doormat, then don't be surprised when they want to wipe their feet on you.

How long do you have to put up with this disrespectful behaviour? For as long as it takes for you to repaint the picture you're projecting. It's smart to realise that you're the author of the way you're treated.

Point of resistance: When you realise that you're not being treated respectfully by someone ... Stop! Assertively state your feelings and if you don't get a satisfactory response, remove yourself from their company and reassess your own behaviour.

## Step 6: Choose Carefully The Company You Keep

Have the people who surround you got your best interests at heart ... or are they draining the life blood out of you? We'll discuss the perils of toxic people in more detail in the Relationship Fitness chapter.

Positive people are like vitamin pills – good for our health; they speak of victories and not defeat, of hope and not despair. Ask them what they think of spring and

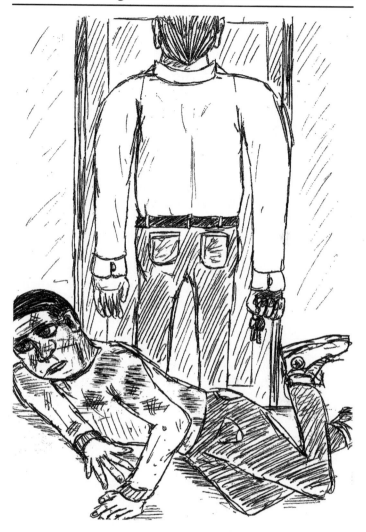

## If you teach people to treat you like a doormat – don't be surprised when they want to wipe their feet on you.

they'll speak positively of it being a time of new growth, new beginnings. They delight in the first buds appearing and the first flowers. Ask them what they think of summer and they'll talk of sunny days, warm evenings, spending time with friends, having barbecues. Ask them what they think of autumn and they'll talk of the pleasure of the children enjoying Hallowe'en and Guy Fawkes Night. Ask them what they think of winter and they talk of Christmas shining like a beacon on the horizon, their thoughts turn to skiing and other pleasurable pursuits that they can only do at this time of year.

Point of resistance: If the people surrounding you are not empowering you ... Stop! Change your company until you meet those who share your positivity.

## Step 7: You Decide Who You Are

You decide who you are. It's your life ... make it count, make it exceptional ... make it extraordinary! When it comes to who you are; IT'S PERSONAL! Never give a second of your time to the people who try to impose their negative opinions on you. Give yourself the power of your own council; you know you better than anyone else. OK, if someone you trust offers some sound advice then there's no reason not to listen, but whether that advice is relevant to you must be decided by you and nobody else.

Point of resistance: When someone tries to place a 'cloak of negative opinion' on your shoulders that you know doesn't fit ... Stop! Reject the cloak, and quietly and persistently carry on reinforcing your own opinions about you that you know are the real truth.

## Step 8: Pay Close Attention To Your Appearance

Select clothes that you know are the ones that make you look and feel good. Also, pay attention to your hair, nails and teeth. Let only the best version of you be presented to the world. You may not be the best-looking but make sure you're looking your best! There's more on appearance in the Physical Fitness chapter.

Point of resistance: If the clothes you're wearing don't make you feel great ... Stop! Remove them from your life completely (not just your wardrobe) and only wear your best.

# Step 9: Exercise, Eat Sensibly And Sleep Well

It's so important to exercise regularly – keeping your body in as good a shape as possible. Also, make sure you're taking in quality nutrition and getting deep, replenishing sleep.

There's more on this in the Physical Fitness chapter.

Point of resistance: Feeling lethargic and out of shape? ... Stop! Start an exercise regime today.

# Step 10: Only Replay Good Memories

Our minds are like those old-fashioned jukeboxes. They contain recordings of all the things that have happened to us over the years. We have a choice as to which recordings we will listen to again and again. It makes sense to only replay the ones we really like ... so, why do so many of us choose to replay recordings that we hate? Things that we did that were embarrassing and we relive the embarrassment. The only good time to relive an embarrassment is if you can look back and laugh at it. We replay times when certain people upset us, and by doing so we relive the upset time and time again. How stupid!

Point of resistance: When a bad recording is about to play ... Stop! Press 'reject' and make a better selection.

Let's use these ten ideas for improving our self-image. By blending them into our everyday routine we'll soon start to see ourselves shining, our speech will become more positive, we'll walk tall, our voice will have more energy and conviction and we'll move with greater purpose. Treat this as a bit of fun and monitor the way you're treated when you display behaviour that's consistent with a person with a positive self-image. You'll be amazed at how well it works. You'll find the new responses you receive will be in line with the new messages you're sending out.

# Confidence

Confidence is about trusting in your own abilities, coupled with an optimistic outlook; it's about being comfortable in your own skin and having a positive perspective on the world. This can result in greater vibrancy and attractiveness, and can even increase your sex appeal. Confident people trust in other people and celebrate their successes as well as their own; they relish new challenges; new ways of expressing themselves – they have plans for the future. When we're feeling confident we tend to express ourselves more clearly in an open and assertive way because we feel valuable, and accepting of ourselves; we're not embarrassed about any weaknesses we have, and we're not afraid to make mistakes – we don't fear failure or worry about what other people think about us. Our self-esteem is healthy.

Is confidence something you can learn? Of course it is … but it does mean getting a grip and taking a reality check. Often people who lack confidence have a faulty mindset, believing that they're just unfortunate and have been dealt the wrong cards in life, and so don't get the breaks, when a healthier way of thinking would be to understand that maybe it's more a question of how we play those cards – improving our skills, so we can play a better game, could be the answer.

Any time we want we can choose to start practising new confident behaviours and disciplines. We just need to look closely at what a confident person is doing differently to us and then use practice and repetition to begin making the components of confidence part of our own reality.

The key to creating confidence is to achieve small victories: select a starting point but instead of aiming for the big prize, just take the first step. We could start by assessing our appearance; what does your dress sense and hair style say about you – do you stand out ... do they project confidence? You could take up a regular exercise programme to improve your fitness levels, maybe by joining a gym? How is your posture; do you walk with purpose? You could work on the melody of your voice and smile more and practise making good eye contact. You could choose to take a greater interest in the people you talk to, and in so doing feel more natural because you've taken the attention off yourself. Sit at the front, take up more space and announce to the world that you've arrived and you're important. Experiment with these suggestions by taking that first step, and then notice the changes in the responses you get from other people.

# "Confidence is about raising the banner of faith in yourself."

© 2014 NJT

# Assertiveness

Assertiveness is about:

- You being comfortable in expressing your opinions and feelings openly to others, without feeling fearful or awkward;

- Feeling comfortable about saying "No";

- Choosing how you're going to spend your time and with whom;

- Not being afraid to ask for what you want;

- Allowing yourself to change your mind without explaining yourself to others;

- Having the right to say 'I don't know' or I don't understand' without feeling stupid or guilty;

- Feeling comfortable in saying "I was wrong" or "I made a mistake";

- Your right to privacy;

- Deciding and sticking to clear boundaries and being confident in defending your position;

- Being able to talk openly about yourself and to listen to others whether you agree with them or not;

- The ability to give positive and negative feedback;

- Expressing a positive and optimistic outlook;

- Being able to accept responsibility;

- Feeling comfortable in delegating to others;

- Always maintaining self-control;

- Always being on equal terms;

- Not exaggerating: sticking to facts.

In brief, assertiveness is about standing up for yourself! It's a grown-up way of behaving.

An assertive voice gets results! Results without giving rise to unwanted emotions, like resentment and anger. By practising assertiveness you're effectively stating that your rights are equal to anyone else's. It's about expressing your thoughts, feelings and beliefs in an honest and appropriate way and also listening to the other person. Being assertive is good for super-charging your self-esteem. It stops anyone from taking advantage of you. Assertiveness is not passive; it's not aggressive, but is a positive force of personality. It's a powerful inter-personal skill. It commands respect! Other people respect you more and you respect yourself more.

Assertiveness is visible:

Your posture is erect but relaxed, you walk with ease and purpose, your facial expressions are calm and thoughtful, you smile and make eye contact and your voice is calm, yet forceful without being too loud or too quiet.

How are others likely to respond to assertive behaviour?

- They'll listen to you.

- They'll admire your self-confidence and self-respect.

- They're more likely to give you what you want.

- They'll see you as an honest, straight-talker who's clear in your objective.

- They'll appreciate you being caring, fair and professional.

- They'll feel empowered by having you around.

- They wouldn't even consider trying to take advantage of you.

...and you?

- You'll feel positive and respected.

- Your self-confidence will be boosted and your self-esteem healthy.

# Passive

Being passive makes you compliant with what other people want. Sometimes it's caused by a strong inner feeling of wanting to be liked by everybody. Passive people often behave the way they do because they don't see themselves as being equal to others and as a result they leave others to take the lead, to take responsibility and make the decisions.

Passive people often put themselves down, which can make them feel inferior and this leads to low self-esteem and low self-confidence, which promotes more passive behaviour which leads to a vicious cycle that's self-perpetuating. A passive person will often speak softly or apologetically, give poor eye contact and display a slumped body posture.

One thing's for sure, passive behaviour always puts you in a position of weakness.

It's good to create an awareness of when we're behaving this way.

Do you say "Yes" when you'd rather say "No" to friends or relatives when they ask a favour of you to do something you really don't want to do? Do you feel awkward and/or afraid about returning a faulty item to a shop for a refund because you feel you might offend the salesperson or be looked upon as being trivial or petty?

Are you afraid to complain about poor service in a restaurant because, once again, you feel the staff may be offended, and may even contaminate your food?

Do you answer your phone and politely listen to some cold caller trying to sell you something you don't want, when you have more important things to do but feel somewhat awkward in stating that you're not interested?

Do you feel irrational fear about dealing with people in authority ... bank managers, doctors etc., placing their heads above yours so that you feel tongue-tied and uncomfortable in expressing yourself?

People who are passive often feel angry and bad about themselves after the event because of the genuine frustration they feel at the difficulty in asserting themselves. They often feel that things are out of their control; they feel helpless and that their needs are not being met. This can manifest in feelings of guilt, blame, anxiety and even depression.

Is there ever a time when passive behaviour is preferable?

Probably the only time would be if you were in a dangerous situation and passive behaviour could be used as a ploy for self-preservation.

Basically, super-assertiveness is what we need because human beings have a subconscious tendency to home in on and attack self-manifested, unsubstantiated weakness (apologetic behaviour that reflects an inferiority complex), so displaying weak passive behaviour can lead to us being treated like a doormat, having our opinions ignored and being spoken to disrespectfully.

# The Supermarket Story

I remember a time when I was shopping in a supermarket and as I approached the checkouts I noticed that there were long queues at all of them. I selected one and joined behind an elderly lady about six people back. She turned to me and said in a very soft and passive voice something about me having less shopping than her and would I like to go ahead of her. I wasn't that fussed as I only had about two items fewer than her anyway but as she spoke she was already physically stepping back behind me, so I just said "OK, thanks."

I carried on waiting; as I did I heard her voice again. Someone else had come along and joined our queue, she said to them the same as she said to me, so I now had someone new standing behind me and she was even further back.

Finally my time came to be served. I paid for my goods, gathered my bags and began to head for the exit, out of curiosity I looked back and saw the elderly lady was now about six people back in a different queue. I wondered what her story was, what had made her feel that everyone else was more important than her. I had visions of her still being there at closing time with her being the last but one customer and waiting for the other person to go ahead of her. That's passive behaviour!

How can we make the change from being passive to being assertive?

If you're someone who always feels nervous and anxious before an act of assertiveness, you should gently introduce the following tips into your daily life by using awareness:

- Use direct eye contact with the person you're talking to, but without staring;

- Regulate your breathing and speak clearly and to

the point – this should allow you to keep a calm tone of voice;

- Never begin with, "I'm sorry but..."
- Be polite but firm;
- Concentrate on staying relaxed, and not getting angry.

Stick to what it is that you want to say and don't let the other person use 'mind force', if they have a more dominant personality, to dissipate your assertiveness by inducing guilt or anger in you. Assertiveness is NOT about being dominant and is a key to good leadership, because it includes and involves people, while dominance often involves bullying.

Use 'I' more than 'you' when asserting yourself: "I feel..."; "I would like to see..."; "I would really appreciate it if..."

If you use 'you' it could be seen as blaming or an attack which wouldn't help you to achieve your objective.

# Aggressive

An aggressive person will often express themselves at the expense of others without consideration for the other person's feelings or whether they themselves are right or wrong. They often have a desire to dominate, and sometimes even humiliate other people.

They'll use an acidic tone of voice, with volume, to intimidate, and body language that's threatening and overbearing, often violating someone's private space. They believe their own opinion is always right.

They can be verbally and physically abusive; criticising, blaming, attacking. Often impulsive and rude, they interrupt without listening to the other person's point of view.

This kind of behaviour reveals that the aggressive person is not that comfortable with what they're saying and doesn't feel that they can express themselves very well in a reasonable and calm way; they appear very tense, resorting to behaviour that's domineering, manipulative and argumentative.

It can be seen as being over the top, violent and even dangerous and it's this kind of behaviour that can often alienate people.

## Passive/Aggressive: The Lethal Combination

Sometimes we will come across people who are passive/aggressive. Usually, this kind of person feels powerless, weak and resentful and doesn't feel that they can deal with you head on. They smile and pretend that everything is OK while secretly trying to undermine you. More often than not their facial expressions don't match how they feel; they often use sarcasm and appear overly cooperative while undermining and disrupting ... and even on occasions using sabotage as a vehicle for their resentment.

A good friend of mine shared a true story with me that formed the basis for his own assertiveness:

# Grandma's Recipe
## (An Assertiveness Technique)

It was a Tuesday morning; my first lesson of the day was geography. I walked into the classroom put my books on the desk and sat down. Suddenly, I was kicked from behind; it was Stephen Hedges, the school bully.

"How's it going big nose, ha ha?" he said, always with that stupid, irritating little laugh.

"What about you, you look as if an elephant's sat on your nose and squashed it?" I replied with force.

He kicked me again...

"I'm going to beat you up at break time, ha ha!"

"You couldn't beat up a mouse, you're the school wimp!" I retorted loudly.

The teacher walked in, the other kids looked at me, shocked at the change in me, the change that had come about since the day before, but had really begun the previous Saturday...

It was on the Saturday that Grandma had come to visit for a week. She was a loud, domineering woman ... and I actually found her a little bit scary! One thing I did like about her, though, was that every time she came to see us she would make the most amazing cake ... it was full of all the best ingredients: there were nuts, cherries, raisins; all the things I loved, and it was absolutely perfect ... every time! The making of her cake became an expected and much-looked-forward-to part of her visits; I'm sure everyone in the family would have been disappointed if she didn't make one.

We would make a special trip to the local supermarket to select the ingredients; Grandma seemed such an expert – she would pick up several packs of raisins, for example, and examine them closely before selecting the one that met her standards and discarding with a casual disdain the ones that didn't.

When we got home she would set out the work surface exactly how she wanted it. There would be the ingredients together in the middle, the mixing bowl in front of me, the baking tin to the left, the scales to the right, and the brown paper bag at the back ... the brown paper...? "Grandma, what's in the brown paper bag?" She would never let me see inside; it was always kept just out of arm's length, and to be absolutely honest I wouldn't have dared to look in it, out of fear of Grandma's wrath. All she would say was, "Never you mind – that's the magic I'll be adding later."

I got to help mix the ingredients and then looked forward to licking the bowl at the end. As soon as I'd finished mixing, Grandma would say, "Turn away now, I'm just going to add the magic." I'd hear the rustling of the brown bag and a glugging of liquid followed by a rapid stirring. "OK, you can turn back now." As I turned back ... Whoa! I was met by the powerful and intoxicating vapours of Grandma's magic potion – I wasn't sure what it was, but it sure made my head spin. The mixture was now ready to go into the tin and then the oven, with the result being this most wonderful aroma wafting through the whole house.

I had many slices over that weekend and even had an extra-large piece put aside for my school lunchbox on Monday morning.

Monday wasn't a good day for me; when I got home my mother could see I'd been crying. "What's the matter?" she said with a look of concern. I couldn't hold back the tears, "It's Stephen Hedges, he keeps kicking me and calling me big nose ... and he stole my piece of Grandma's cake." Mother sighed as if she thought, "Is that all it's about?" "Just ignore him; I've told you before, it's the only way." With that she left the room to continue her chores. Grandma was sitting over at the side of the room, listening intently.

"Come and sit down ... NOW LISTEN TO ME ... EVERY TIME YOU ALLOW THIS STUPID BOY'S BEHAVIOUR TO AFFECT YOU, IT SHOWS UP IN YOUR VOICE AND YOU SOUND TIMID. EVERY TIME YOU LET THIS NONSENSE PENETRATE YOUR MIND, IT SHOWS UP IN YOUR POSTURE AND YOUR SHOULDERS SLUMP. EVERY SINGLE TIME THAT YOU LET THIS POISON BREACH YOUR DEFENCES, IT SHOWS UP IN YOUR FOCUS AND YOU ONLY SEE

THE NEGATIVE. You're like a ship on the ocean; all the time that the water is on the outside, you're floating, but when it gets on the inside, you're sinking. YOUNG MAN, YOU NEED TO RECLAIM YOUR POWER. Sometimes, like your mother said, you can ignore these people and they'll go away. BUT SOMETIMES THEY DON'T and you have to THROW IT BACK WITH FIRE ... THROW IT BACK WITH FIRE, DO YOU UNDERSTAND ME?"

I could hardly speak ... "Ye... yes, Grandma," I stuttered.

She continued, "Your mind, like Grandma's cake, only deserves the best ingredients; we have a choice to what we put in ..." she lowered her voice and lent towards me and said, "And that's Grandma's recipe," she paused ... and then got up from her chair and walked out of the room.

I stood rooted to the spot; all I could think of were Grandma's words echoing in the recesses of my mind; "THROW IT BACK WITH FIRE, THROW IT BACK WITH FIRE."

It was a Tuesday morning, my first lesson of the day was geography, I walked into the classroom put my books on the desk and sat down. Suddenly, I was kicked from behind; it was Stephen Hedges the school bully.

"How's it going big nose ha ha?" he said, always with that stupid, irritating little laugh.

"What about you, you look as if an elephant's sat on your nose and squashed it?" I replied with force.

He kicked me again...

"I'm going to beat you up at break time, ha ha!"

"You couldn't beat up a mouse, you're the school wimp!" I retorted loudly.

The teacher walked in, the other kids looked at me shocked, at the change in me, the change that had come

about since the day before but had really begun the previous Saturday … when Grandma came to visit and I
learnt all about her amazing recipe.

# Enthusiasm

I've heard enthusiasm described as your 'psychological
ignition system' but my favourite description is 'divine
transport'. That says it all! It can carry you along like a
magical force – an invisible energy that you can't touch,
taste or smell but you know it's there when somebody
has it. It's that certain thing that gets you out of bed in
the morning with that rise-and-shine feeling. With this
powerful life force coursing through your body it can
make a difference in every area of your life.

Enthusiasm and action are like perfect partners, with both
needed when aspiring to a life of success, and the more of
these two fellows you can muster up the more likely you're
to achieve your dreams. Enthusiasm is a key ingredient
that won't allow you to quit; instead, it empowers you to
take the necessary risks that may be required for you to
reach your goal, overriding minor irritations, fears and
worries that may otherwise hold you back.

Without doubt, it separates champions from the medi-
ocre, and when I say champions, I'm not just talking
about a select few who have become champions in some
honourable pursuit; I'm talking at a more grass-roots
level, about you being a champion of you, me being a
champion of me, rating ourselves – being the best we
can possibly be, and being proud of who we are.

Enthusiasm is faith and excitement in advance – born
from the anticipation of something that inspires and
delights you. It shows the world that you're sold on life,
a participator rather than a spectator, a life affirmer
rather than a denier. It's a very positive and infectious
personality trait, so how can we bring enthusiasm into
our lives, if we don't already have it?

# Step 1: Gratitude

Be grateful for all the good things that are in your life already ... the things that you may take for granted: your health, your family, friends, a roof over your head, food in the cupboard, living in a great country ... I'm sure you could suggest many more. Think for a moment how blessed you are with these positives in your life and how impoverished you would be without them.

# Step 2: Voice

Put enthusiasm in your voice. Uplift yourself and others with positive and enthusiastic words. Paint bright, vivid pictures in the minds of those you come into contact with. Let them remember you as a person who talks of the good things in life: of victories not defeats, of love not hate.

# Step 3: Smile

Manifest enthusiasm with an infectious smile. Let your aliveness shine out from every pore on your face. A big smile can light up a room and change the collective mood of everyone in it. There's more about the power of a smile in the Physical Fitness chapter.

# Step 4: Speed It Up

Speed it up, life it up, life up your movements. A person with enthusiasm moves in a certain way – they move with purpose and energy. Take advice from William Shakespeare: "Assume a virtue if you have it not." This is known as the "as if" principle which requires that you act as if you're already in possession of the attribute that you desire. By practising it persistently it will become your natural behaviour. Visualise clearly this attribute, and the person you'd like to be, and incorporate that awareness into your everyday thinking. All it takes is commitment and focus, and a desire to succeed.

## Step 5: Knowledge

Build enthusiasm through knowledge. What subjects get you really excited? Select those which interest you the most and make a decision to learn as much as you can, maybe even becoming something of an expert on the things that really fire you up. The more you learn, the more your enthusiasm will start growing and flowing at a rapid rate.

## Step 6: Enthuse Others

Help others become enthusiastic by encouraging and supporting them. Remember, enthusiasm can be infectious and by nourishing someone else's self-esteem you'll automatically nourish your own. It's just as easy to say a kind word as it is to criticise and complain, so make sure your words are musical notes from a symphony and not acid rain.

## Step 7: Resign As The Chief Burden-Bearer Of The Universe

You don't need to get exasperated by the problems of the world and carry them around on your shoulders, especially when so many of them are out of your control. You can be sure that governments will always do things that are unpopular; this will never change, but you can choose your own attitude and decide to exercise a degree of detachment. Accepting external things that we can't change doesn't mean we agree with them, but by resisting what is outside of our control will only make us miserable. Lighten up and be the best version of you, lead by example, and do the best you can and live a life of purpose.

# "Enthusiasm is faith and excitement in advance – born from the anticipation of something that inspires and delights you."

© 2014 NJT

## Goals

What are your goals? Do you want to get promoted in a job? Do you want to attract new clients to your business? Do you have plans that involve exercising or losing weight? Do you want to get a book published? Do you want to meet someone special? Well, the fact that you're reading this book tells me that there's a good chance that one of your goals is to go from being an excuse-maker to a life-maker.

It's important that your goals excite you and motivate you ... they must initiate pictures in your mind of you being in a much better place after you've accomplished them.

When you begin your journey to accomplishing a specific goal, it must be something that's self-motivating, that energises you and electrifies you; success will then be much, much more likely.

Setting powerful goals that challenge us can boost us in every area of our lives, thus increasing our self-esteem and self-confidence, because most people, I believe, are switched on by success and by living a life fully activated.

It's important that we set short-term, mid-term and long-term goals as by differentiating between sizes of goal helps us to be realistic and avoid losing motivation: if the goal is really big and we spend too much time focusing on the outcome rather than the journey we can easily be daunted and lose our drive to accomplish it. Even though it's good to be aware of the big picture and to see a vivid result with all the benefits you'll receive once the goal is achieved, the focus must be directed towards the first stepping stone. It's about taking baby steps.

Always write your goals down and only share them with people who you know will support you.

Here are 4 steps to get things moving:

**Step 1:**  *Be crystal clear in what you want to achieve.*

**Step 2:**  *Break your path down into mini-goals: stepping stones.*

**Step 3:**  *Visualise your whole being integrated with that which you want to become.*

**Step 4:**  *Bring on the 'A' word: Action! – The magic word in all success!*

Keep checking on the progress you're making – you're more likely to maintain momentum if you check it regularly.

If at any time you're unhappy with the progress you're making towards your goal, you need to assess it carefully and honestly to see what's holding you back. Personally I like to consult with someone positive who I can trust to give me constructive feedback. This helps immensely, especially if, for example, it's a writing project and I'm looking for a fresh angle – it can be so beneficial to have a strong, motivated companion on my side to help and encourage me if things are moving slower than I'd like. This strategy can be helpful for everyone, and once we start to make progress again, I believe we should honour and reward ourselves for every success we achieve on our mission to reach our goal – celebrate each milestone reached.

Never feel awkward or unhappy if you feel you have to change your goal in any way, because often, as time moves on things do need changing and updating. Your time is better spent on achieving than it is on beating yourself up because you haven't made as much progress as you would have liked or things haven't moved on as quickly as you would have wanted.

People often postpone the things they really want to do in life because it's too easy to get immersed in the excuse-making process – they question whether the goal is worthy or whether they themselves are worthy – and end up not doing anything.

Goals give us targets to aim for – and we like targets, because all the time we've got something to shoot at, it keeps us going ... it keeps us in the loop.

Often when we work on a worthwhile project that has taken some time and has seen us happily absorbed, we reach the end and can't wait to get started on the next one.

We must be careful, however, that we don't select too many goals or ones that are unrealistic. We must prioritise, because too many will mean we're spreading ourselves too thinly and will probably end up not being very successful. Unrealistic ones will lead us to a land of false hope and ultimate disappointment.

Some people set personal goals, career goals and business goals with all the best intentions and then everything goes wrong. If we don't attack our goals with the right attitude we can end up wasting our time and undermining our success and then become cynical and demotivated.

# "Use the desire in your present to put the promise in your future."

© 2014 NJT

## Fully Spiritual

Being spiritual can be of amazing benefit to you in revealing to you who you really are. By trusting your inner knowing you're allowing your life to be directed by your own power. Spirituality means "of the spirit or soul" as opposed to material or physical things. It means coming home to your true self ... your spiritual essence.

A spiritual person always endeavours to be their best; in their thoughts, words and in their actions – whether they're conversing with strangers, cleaning their house or driving a car, whatever they're doing, wherever they may be, they live by a certain standard.

If your speech is dotted with profanities and you gossip about others, always spreading bad news; if your actions are harmful to others and to the environment then your spirit will be tarnished and so will your life be. You'll need to purge your body and soul, listen to your heart and raise your thoughts to a new level.

A spiritual person, often creative, is wholeheartedly dedicated to their calling, to their passion – never counting the hours or days, because time isn't important; it's their mission, their work that's important. By adopting this attitude and immersing themselves in their journey with a certain detachment as to the final outcome, they're more able to move towards their goals fearlessly and unencumbered. They're accepting and understanding of the fact that they can be affected by problems as much as everyone else, the difference being they're in a more secure and enlightened place personally and so are more able to deal with these problems as they arise, without being cowed or derailed by them. They believe strongly that things will always work out for their greater benefit in the end. This belief enables them to keep things more in perspective than others might.

Some people may work in a job where they spend a lot of time looking at the clock, thinking of ways to 'kill time', seeing their day as an endurance test. When we allow time and certain expectations to control our lives we become nothing more than slaves to 'time and reward' but when one is occupied with a labour of love, time has no meaning; in fact, sometimes it may appear to no longer exist.

When we look at the lives of great leaders in history, we can see that their work lives on long after they have passed, because their efforts had their heart and soul in them ... their spirit. Even when they experienced trouble and rejection they still carried on because their spirit was greater than their problems or the opinions of their detractors.

A spiritual person will live by their own inner guidance system, and this system is your spiritual centre of excellence and it communicates with you in many ways: have you ever had a feeling – an inner warning of sorts – not to do something, but you went ahead and did it anyway only to achieve a negative result and you saying to yourself, "I knew I should have followed my gut." That inner knowing is there for a reason – don't ignore it.

You can receive messages through your thoughts and feelings, and the environment: thoughts that are constantly repeating and feelings that won't go away and through subtle messages from unexpected places: something you may read; something someone says.

A spiritual person has an inclusive and enquiring approach to life. They're broad-minded and tolerant, and will consider issues from many viewpoints; never becoming negatively opinionated because someone's of a different colour or religion. They respect the rights of others to be whom and what they are and to follow their own path. A spiritual person will comfortably walk with anyone from any race or religion, of any sexual orientation or with any ability or disability: they're human beings who connect with other human beings. They always find the strength to lift the fallen, to wipe the tears from the sad and to give direction to the lost.

A spiritual person has a heart filled with joy. They recognise their joy even when the sunshine has given way to a storm or when they suffer a defeat ... even when they're not feeling too well.

They always remain level-headed, never showing off or showing fanaticism; in fact, they never have to advertise their spirituality because others are aware of it by the way they live their lives. Some may believe they're a soft touch; easy to take advantage of ... but No! They fight for what they believe in, not for self-gain but for the common good – they're proud to set an example.

A fully spiritual person will always strive to find balance within themselves and in all things.

- They're at peace with themselves.

- Their words and actions have synergy.

- They're non-judgemental, e.g. they're indifferent to physical appearance.

- They're unconditionally loving.

- They'll always seek to share their light and positivity with the world.

- They respect themselves and others.

- They don't gossip or talk badly about others.

- They never intentionally hurt or do harm to others or the environment.

- They're always present and live in the now.

- They never give up.

- They're never self-righteous lecturers.

- They believe in equality and justice.

- They practise humility at all times.

- They show compassion and forgiveness at all times.

- They believe in continuous learning and self-improvement.

- They invite beauty into their lives at every opportunity.

Awareness of your spirituality gives you greater clarity when it comes to knowing yourself, by the:

- Recognition of what makes you happy;

- Recognition of 'perfect' moments: children laughing, the kiss of a gentle breeze, birds singing, the smell of flowers;

- Recognition of acts of kindness that happen during your day;

- Recognition of positive events in your life;

- Appreciation of inspiring literature that raises your vibration.

Your spirituality represents joy, peace and love, when you:

- Know you're on your correct path;

- Trust and follow the knowing that you have in your heart;

- Trust that inner voice;

- Trust that inner feeling;

- Find ways to earn a living doing what you love to do.

To have a successful life you must live from within and be true to who you really are. You can try looking outside yourself for happiness but you'll never find it, because to rely on the physical world, and materialism and its potentially transient pleasures to create lasting happiness, can leave you disappointed ... although as outside stimuli they may press your inner 'happy buttons', but on some occasions, although not all, the feeling may be short-lived and often leave you unfulfilled.

In the Physical Fitness chapter we'll look closely at meditation, because meditation is our spiritual listening system. It's the best way of tuning into that inner wisdom. It allows you to quiet the mind and clear away the daily noise.

Trust the universe, trust your inner knowing – sometimes it can be difficult, but persevere – the results will be the right results, and worth it.

# Mental Fitness Action Invitation

Below are vital ingredients that when added to all the other ingredients in the PLB Code mixing bowl, and worked on consistently, will lead you towards being the excuse-free success you've always wanted to be. It's about creating daily disciplines of action to create momentum.

Decide to:

- Use positive vocabulary – to bring sunshine into people's lives.

- Develop a winning attitude and a broad smile by immersing yourself in a positive environment.

- Use positive self-talk – be your own best friend and life coach.

- Go inwards to your spiritual hub to consult your intuition when making an important decision.

- Select an unproductive habit that doesn't serve you and replace it.

- Work on your self-image – by focusing on your good points.

- Select goals – it's always better to have something challenging to aim for, rather than just drifting.

- Get enthusiastic about something to add fire to your life.

- Select a time to experiment with a new assertiveness technique – have fun with this one – if you give it all you've got, you'll be amazed at the results.

- Sky-rocket your self-esteem by working on some or all of the above, and you'll find that each small success will boost your confidence.

# Chapter 3

## THE PLB CODE

# PHYSICAL FITNESS

Ye Olde Scroll

THE
VEHICLE

THE STUDENT

# Exercise

**I can't stress enough the benefits of exercise –
They're immense! There are so many ailments
against which exercise can help to guard you,
such as heart disease, strokes and diabetes to
name but a few. It can also help to slow the effects of osteoporosis ... and some cancers; in
some cases, lowering your chances of contrac-
tion by as much as 50% and lowering the risk of
early death by as much as 30%. Plus, when you
think about it, exercise is an easy-to-take 'medicine' that you can take any time you choose.**

I'm not sure that I would describe exercise as a miracle
cure – after all, what is? – but it's a prevention platform
that's always available, if you choose to engage with it –
and if you forget your dose, it's easy to correct and get
back on track. It really is a potent tool that can lead to a
happier and healthier life.

Apart from reducing the chances of developing certain
serious illnesses it also has numerous other benefits,
such as: boosting your self-esteem, improving your
self-image, lifting your mood, strengthening your immune system, facilitating better and deeper sleeping,
giving you more energy, aiding better love-making –
and that's not all; it can also reduce your risk of stress,
depression, anxiety, high blood pressure, and developing dementia and Alzheimer's disease – it really is a
'system energiser'.

Using moderate intensity aerobic (cardiovascular) exercises (toning exercises), that are strenuous enough to
raise your heart rate and make you sweat, can be a great
place to start. These could include: running, jogging,
walking, Nordic walking, dancing, swimming, cycling,
skipping, stair climbing, rowing, circuit training, using
a treadmill, playing games such as tennis or badminton.

After raising our fitness levels using some of the above, we can start to work on some anaerobic exercises (strength training) to strengthen and build our muscles; these exercises are usually short and vigorous with high intensity – we could include: weight training; sprinting; jumping, including long jump and high jump; push-ups and pull-ups.

Other physical activities we can engage in that can be incredibly beneficial to our wellbeing are the ones which involve our flexibility, including: stretching, Yoga, Pilates and Tai Chi.

Stretching can be beneficial as it increases the flexibility of and movement in our joints; it can help increase blood flow to the muscles, thus shortening our recovery time from injuries. It can be beneficial to your posture, minimising aches and pains; it can relieve stress from tight and tense muscles; and it can improve our coordination and balance, helping us to stay more physically vital as we age.

Yoga has been proven to help with the relief of arthritis, depression and irritable bowel syndrome. It can help create a healthy body through a healthy mind, especially when used in conjunction with meditation – improving memory and awareness, boosting our immune system and slowing the ageing process.

Pilates can be great for posture and balance, focusing on core strength. It encourages the use of deep breathing for greater lung capacity and better circulation and can aid endurance and fluidity of movement.

Tai Chi is great for creating balance, and strengthening our reflexes. It's also great for relaxation, for concentration and better sleep.

In our modern world more and more people are starting to get the exercise bug. They're experiencing a shift in their mindset and realising that an exercise routine is an intelligent and smart thing to do. It becomes more important if you have a job that's mainly sedentary: where you're seated at a computer all day or driving, for example, and then come home and sit again to watch TV or play computer games ... weight gain can become an issue, sometimes, in exceptional cases, leading to obesity.

Being inactive is the silent assassin – and yet is so easy to correct. Spending long periods of time sitting or lying down is not conducive to a long and healthy life – it's not what our bodies are designed for, and it's why I call the Physical Fitness area of the PLB Code the Vehicle because it's all about movement, and that's what our bodies should be doing ... moving!

We need to reduce our sedentary behaviour as much as possible. I once asked the people at the CN Tower in Toronto if I could take the stairs... (Unfortunately they said "No.")

It's time to throw away the excuses and realise that it's pretty cool to be fit – it shows self-respect!

# "Exercise is an easy-to-take medicine that always makes you feel better."

© 2014 NJT

# Nutrition

A healthy body, like a healthy mind is the direct result of what we put in. If we put in quality nutrition then the chances of us living a long and pain-free life are dramatically increased. None of us will ever be likely to find a fountain of youth to drink from, but with careful thought and planning, I believe we can stay fitter and stronger than previous generations. There's definitely a new mindset when it comes to what we're capable of doing as we age – I firmly believe that thinking has changed since the middle of the last century and what has been said about 50 being the new 30 and 60 being the new 40 is true.

We're living in the information age where gaining knowledge about living intelligently and smart is very easy – we just need to choose positive daily disciplines where exercise and nutrition are foremost in our minds.

I would like to share with you my personal top twenty superfood 'must haves' in a healthy diet and why.

## 1. Broccoli

Apart from being a delicious and easily prepared vegetable to cook and eat, broccoli is said to contain almost twice as much vitamin C as an orange, is rich in calcium (strong bones) and contains selenium, a mineral that's believed to have anti-cancer and anti-viral properties. It's also a good source of folate, a naturally occurring folic acid that can help prevent heart disease, and has an anti-oxidant called lutein that can slow down age-related macular degeneration (AMD), a condition that causes impaired vision and blindness mainly in people over 60.

## 2. Garlic

Garlic really is a superfood: it's been popular for thousands of years and has amazing health benefits; it contains heaps of healthy chemicals, including many antioxidants which make it a powerful anti-ageing food. This natural wonder is believed to fight heart disease, cancers, high blood pressure, blood clotting, and even calm stress and regulate mood swings ... and is so versatile – it can be consumed raw or cooked, or even in odourless capsule form without any anti-social side effects.

# 3. Tomatoes (non-GM)

Tomatoes are another amazing and versatile food that, like broccoli, are a great source of vitamin C, especially in the soft tissue that surrounds the seeds. The tomato is also a great source for vitamin A (for good eyesight) and B-complex (for energy levels), potassium (for blood pressure) and phosphorus (for cellular reproduction). They're also rich in lycopene, flavonoids and other phytochemicals with anti-carcinogenic (anti-cancer) properties. Love that love apple!

# 4. Oats

A bowl of porridge oats can be a great way of starting the day, especially when it's supplemented with fruits, nuts and honey. Oats contain a soluble fibre called beta-glucan that can be very effective in lowering cholesterol which is vitally important as high cholesterol levels are connected to the build-up of plaque in the arteries which can lead to heart attacks and strokes.

Oats can also enhance the immune system and help stabilise blood sugar levels, thus reducing the risk of type 2 diabetes. They're also great for the digestive system, allowing for the smooth and effective removal of waste materials. They're a great source of essential vitamins vital for good health and longevity: B1 (thiamin), B7 (biotin), and vitamin E, plus zinc, selenium, iron, manganese and magnesium. Are you getting your oats?

# 5. Eggs

Eggs are such an amazing, inexpensive food that it would be difficult to imagine living without them. We boil, fry, scramble and poach them, make them into omelettes, and even bake them. We use them in cake-making and countless other ways; they're protein rich, supplying important amino acids and a whole bundle of vitamins including A, E, and vitamins B2 (riboflavin), B6 (pyridoxine), B9 (folic acid), and B12 (cobalamin).

# 6. Honey

Honey really is liquid gold, a fabulous natural sweetener with far fewer calories than normal sugar and it's been used for centuries. It's rich in the B vitamins – B1 (thiamin), B2 (riboflavin), B3 (niacin) and B5 (pantothenic acid) – contains no cholesterol and has very little sodium. It's a food that the body likes, it's gentle on the digestive system and when combined with porridge oats, this great source of carbohydrates makes for a seriously nourishing and energy-boosting experience. It has antioxidants that promote healthy skin and restorative sleep.

# 7. Baked Beans

A much loved family favourite for many, many years, made with wholesome haricot beans and a rich sauce. They're a great source of fibre which is important for keeping your intestines working properly. The fibre also helps lower cholesterol, reducing the risk of heart disease.

They're rich in protein – an important muscle and strength builder – and are also a great source of iron, manganese, magnesium, potassium and vitamins B6 and B9. They have high levels of antioxidants, helping fight the free radicals (highly reactive oxygen-based molecules that have a negative effect on whatever they come into contact with) in the body and cutting the risk of some cancers and other illnesses. They're also good for hair and nail health.

# 8. Onions

When you're cutting an onion you have every reason for tears: tears of joy – onions really are something when it comes to your health. They're rich in quercetin and chromium: the first is a powerful antioxidant that combats a variety of illnesses; the latter helps maintain a proper hormonal balance in the body. They're another food that's great for encouraging the growth of good bacteria in the digestive system, helping it to function properly. They're of their most beneficial when eaten raw.

# 9. Asparagus

Asparagus is a member of the lily family. It's considered to be an excellent body detoxifier. It has many similar qualities to some of the superfoods we've already looked at, such as cutting the risk of heart disease and some cancers, but it also has another quality: it's seen as being an aphrodisiac...

It's also one of the best providers of vitamin K which promotes normal blood clotting. It can also protect against bone fractures and the calcification of arteries; it may also offer some resistance to liver cancer and prostate cancer.

# 10. Salmon

Here's yet another fabulous superfood, probably one of the best you can have. It's great for cardiovascular health and for muscle development. Salmon is high in omega-3 fatty acids which can give you increased energy and an upbeat mood ... and that much valued feeling of wellbeing.

These omega-3 fatty acids can be beneficial to brain function, aiding better memory. As part of a healthy diet they can reduce the risk of developing Parkinson's disease or Alzheimer's.

On a lighter note, salmon consumption can give you lovely, shiny hair, healthy skin and brighter eyes.

## 11.  Cinnamon

This gorgeous and aromatic spice packs a mighty punch in the health department. In past studies it has been found to slow the proliferation of cancer cells, help regulate blood sugar levels, reduce the chances of diabetes and play a major role in good cardiovascular health. It's also noted as being good for memory and overall cognitive functioning.

## 12.  Ginger

This natural anti-inflammatory agent is an amazing food for relieving the symptoms of sickness, indigestion and diarrhoea. It can also minimise the effects of respiratory conditions, colds, flu and allergies. It improves the body's absorption and assimilation of essential nutrients.

## 13.  Natural Yogurt

Is another 'easy' food that's very gentle on the digestive system. No wonder it contributes to colon health. It can be beneficial in two ways: firstly, it contains lacto bacteria, a very intestinal-friendly bacteria that promotes a healthy colon; secondly, it's rich in calcium which reduces the risk of polyp formation that can lead to colorectal cancer.

Yogurt can boost immunity – the bacterial cultures help stimulate infection-fighting white blood cells in the blood stream. It's also seen as a great 'healing food' and like oats can be very good for people suffering from stomach upsets and diarrhoea.

## 14.  Apples

Apples contain many benefits for health. Like onions, they contain quercetin that can protect the body from the free radicals that can lead to Alzheimer's disease. They contain pectin that supplies the body with galacturonic acid, lowering the need for insulin, thus helping with the control of diabetes. Pectin is also good for lowering levels of bad cholesterol. Another important component is boron, which is good for strengthening the bones and can reduce the effects of asthma.

## 15.  Plain Chocolate

Plain chocolate enhances your mood due to it containing theobromine and caffeine which are stimulants; it can give you a feeling of pleasure as it encourages the production of endorphins.

It contains a greater percentage of the cocoa bean than milk chocolate making it richer in phytonutrients and antioxidants which are good for cardiovascular function and preventing degenerative diseases. The nitric oxide found in dark chocolate reduces blood pressure and balances the body's hormonal system. It also contains less sugar, more cholesterol-neutral fat and more cocoa polyphenols in a more bioavailable way than milk chocolate.

## 16.  Tea

Tea has many health enhancing properties, such as reducing the risk of heart disease and some cancers.

The antioxidants found in tea are flavonoids, powerful compounds that scientists believe are instrumental in fighting disease. It's believed that the antioxidant levels in tea are more powerful than those found in fruit and vegetables – one cup of tea supplies 200mg of flavonoids.

Both black and green teas are rich in sources of potassium and manganese, as well as vitamin A which has protective properties, vitamin B6, an essential contributor to your body's metabolism, and vitamins B1 and B2 which release energy from food. The potassium is vital for maintaining a normal heartbeat, enabling nerves and muscles to function properly and regulating the fluid level in cells. The manganese is essential for bone growth and overall body development. Five cups a day provide you with around 45% of your daily requirement.

Tea is only a mild diuretic so can be great for your water intake – so my advice is: Get the kettle on!

## 17.    Peanut Butter

Peanut butter is a great source of fibre which is good for controlling blood sugar levels and also cholesterol. It's very high in protein and contains vitamins E and B3 and the minerals potassium and calcium. It has proven to be beneficial in the prevention of gallstones.

## 18.    Olive Oil

Olive oil is a truly amazing product. It's rich in 'good fats', rather than trans fats, and these 'good fats' are great for your cholesterol levels and for your heart.

It boosts your immune system, protects against viruses, reduces systolic and diastolic blood pressure, slows arthritis and increases bone calcification.

It's also rich in vitamin E and in antioxidants that fight against damage caused by free radicals.

## 19.    Nuts

Nuts are another food that can reduce the risk of heart disease and diabetes.

Brazil nuts, for example, contain selenium, an antioxidant that fights the free radicals that cause cancer. They also contain protein, copper, magnesium and vitamin E (for healthy skin).

A handful of cashew nuts a day can help prevent any deficiency diseases by boosting your system with an abundant supply of essential vitamins and minerals. They're heart-friendly as they help increase levels of good cholesterol and lower the levels of bad cholesterol. Their magnesium content helps improve blood flow.

Hazelnuts are often looked upon as one of the healthiest nuts to eat and also one of the most delicious – is there a more desirable nut than a roasted hazelnut?

They can help with weight loss because they stimulate your metabolism, the result being you burn more calories. Also with the high level of unsaturated fats, fibre and protein they make you feel fuller quicker so you're less likely to snack on less healthy alternatives.

# 20. Water

Water is extremely important for maintaining body temperature. It's responsible for the movement of nutrients around the system, for digestion, blood circulation and the excretion of waste.

Generally, your body can survive around thirty days without food but only about a week without water. A loss of around 10% of your water could lead to some very severe ailments and a 20% loss could result in your death.

During the course of a day your body loses vital fluids through respiration, perspiration and excretion, so it's crucial that you keep your water levels replenished. When you become dehydrated your body temperature tends to rise, as does your heart rate. The body has a built-in mechanism to prevent dehydration – when your water levels start to drop too low a message is sent to the brain which activates the sensation of thirst, which is how we monitor how much water we need in our system, and when. Ideally, we should maintain our fluid levels such that we don't reach a point beyond feeling mildly thirsty, as thirst itself indicates too-low levels and the start of dehydration. However, it's important that we're mindful of how much water our bodies need, because flooding our system can be as harmful as becoming dehydrated; too much water will end up depleting our bodies of vital minerals. As such, this is one area where balance is a key word.

There's no definitive amount of water that you should drink because people come in different shapes and sizes, and a larger, heavier person would need to drink a lot more than a smaller, lighter person. You need to listen to your body, and an intelligent path here would be to drink sufficient water to prevent thirst, but also to include in your diet regular quantities of water-rich foods such as fruit and vegetables; as a healthy diet with sufficient water intake can slow down the build-up of toxins in the body that come about not only through what we eat but by the stress levels we endure.

A healthy diet also aids circulation and joint lubrication, lessening the development of certain cancers, stopping constipation, reducing the chance of kidney stones and even helping to reduce the risk of blood clots.

The colour of your urine can be an accurate guide to whether your water intake is adequate.

**Clear**    *you're well hydrated and don't need anything extra at the moment.*

**Pale**    *but with a light yellow hue – some of the waste products in your body have now become visible, but there's no cause for alarm.*

**Bright yellow**    *likely to be the colour of your urine first thing in the morning after sleeping, and not drinking for many hours. Time to reach for a glass of water.*

**Dark
yellow**   *you're dehydrated and could be physically and mentally under stress. Your kidneys are in need of copious amounts of water so they can effectively rid your body of toxins.*

**Red /
Brown**   *eating foods like beetroot can temporarily make your urine run red. Jaundice, due to blood or liver disorders, can turn urine brown. It would be sensible to seek medical advice, if only for peace of mind.*

# Junk Food

It's wise to include as many of my suggested top twenty foods in your diet as possible. Of course, there are many others that may be your own personal favourites and only you can decide which ones are right for you.

I think that if we discipline ourselves to consume mostly the high-quality, life-promoting foods, then there's no real problem if we occasionally give in to temptation and consume some 'junk food'.

I'm not someone who believes that you should never drink cola or eat crisps or sweets; I just believe these items – often referred to as 'empty calories', as they give us little in terms of nutrition – should only be consumed occasionally.

It's sensible to dig a little deeper when it comes to what we eat, and take a greater interest in your own wellbeing; do some research and find out what energises the body and what pollutes it. Really it's about showing yourself some self-respect.

# Alcohol

I'm sure that most of us at one time or another has felt the effects of alcohol – more so when we were young, because more often than not, at a young age we're just not clued up on quality living. I could tell you a story or two of my own concerning my experiences of too much alcohol – you'd probably be quite shocked, as it wouldn't make pretty reading, so I'll spare you the gory details. It's very clear that the effects of over-consumption can be quite negative, especially in terms of accidents, the crime rate, your dignity ... and let's not forget the healthy functioning of your liver.

I'm certainly not advocating that everyone should give up alcohol – far from it; it can be extremely pleasant to enjoy a glass of wine, a bottle of beer, a fine malt whisky or a delicious liquor especially if, like me, you enjoy social occasions. It's about exercising control over your own mind – you making decisions for you and not giving in to peer pressure and having 'one for the road'. Unlike smoking, which has no benefits at all, there are without doubt certain benefits derived from a moderate alcohol intake. I've heard stories of people, 100 years old or older suggesting the reason for their longevity was down to an occasional glass of red wine or brandy.

However, there's no way you can make the most of your life if you mess up your system by excessive alcohol consumption, so let's keep the balance and keep control!

By following the PLB Code you'll find it much easier to handle the negative down times that we all have occasionally, which means you should never feel the urge to 'drown your sorrows' with alcohol – sorrows don't need drowning, they need handling and dealing with, with a clear and rational mind.

# Body Language

What is body language? It's the art of non-verbal communication – comprising posture, gestures and facial expressions, including eye movements, smiles, frowns, head nods, shoulder shrugs and more. It's about body signals, voluntary and involuntary – it's a window to your state of mind.

When we interact with others, we undoubtedly want to be seen as being confident and worthy of respect. I don't think anyone would want to be seen as nervous or looking defeated.

## Posture

Our body posture is a powerful indicator for how we're perceived by others. If we want to create the best impression right from the start we need to stand up straight – stand up and be counted – while keeping a relaxed fluidity to our movements so we don't end up standing out for the wrong reasons, by looking so stiff and starchy it looks as if we're impersonating a plank of wood.

If we stand hunched when we speak, it gives the impression that we don't believe in what we're saying – and if we don't believe it nobody else will. Shrinking, making yourself seem smaller, avoiding eye contact and bowing your head sends the message that you don't feel worthy – and as a result is likely to lose you the respect of other people, and once that respect has been lost it can be extremely difficult to regain. If you want an idea of how an impressive posture can have maximum effect, look at people who have to appear powerful and authoritative as part of their job: policemen, military officers, headmasters, nightclub doormen ... You'd expect them to stand tall with their shoulders back and chests out. You wouldn't expect to see a policeman walking along with his head down, shoulders slumped with a defeated look on his face, because it's behaviour that wouldn't work in that profession.

## Eye Contact

Making good eye contact is an important component of body language, helping you engage with people – it can convey many different messages: playful flirtation with somebody you fancy; showing an employee that you mean business; showing a friend that you care and understand; it can also help calm potentially hostile situations. Good eye contact shows that you're interested in what the other person is saying. It shows respect and good manners and is completely different to staring which can appear creepy, and even threatening. If you feel uncomfortable maintaining direct eye contact, try looking at the bridge of the person's nose or between their eyes.

## The Power Of The Smile

On a global scale what do smiles represent? They represent kindness, warmth, friendliness, lack of hostility, trust and likeability and can be contagious – they have the power to change the collective mood and energy of a room.

A friendly, natural and sincere smile comes from the whole face; the eyes as well as the mouth and cheeks. Born from happy thoughts and wellbeing it's a universal welcome, and generally will be received and responded to as such. An infectious smile can have an effect like the sun shining through a gap in the clouds.

Our smiles can be great assets – they carry a power of their own – they can make us more attractive. A genuine smile radiates positive energy and makes people want to be part of your world: it's a powerful tool for persuading people onto your side and achieving what you want in life. It should be a visible component in your body language armoury.

Smile when you use the phone; people have an uncanny ability to 'see' when someone is smiling on the phone – it's a connection tool that builds rapport and wins friends.

It can be easy to spot a fake smile – sometimes we just know on a subconscious level when it's not for real due to certain 'tells' in someone's facial expressions. Unfortunately, some people are just not very good at faking it; they come across as insincere, it may look forced and/or overdone; almost too enthusiastic, and as a result it can send the opposite message for that which was intended.

People meeting you for the first time subconsciously make a judgement about you within the first few seconds of setting eyes on you, so what better way is there of making a positive impression than showing off your pearly whites?

Who has the most genuine smiles? Children! It's likely to be because they haven't developed any worries in life, so their smiles are usually true and natural.

A smile can boost your self-esteem by sending a message to your subconscious that you're content and like yourself. It can also boost your sex appeal because more often than not people are attracted to those who exude joy or a sense of fun. As such, you can often make yourself and others feel better just by smiling – try experimenting when you're feeling gloomy, and see the effect that the physical act of smiling has on your mood, and potentially on others people's moods too.

A genuine smile talks – it says: I'm so happy to see you, I'm really glad you're here. It brings sunshine to the sad and comfort to the lives of those who are feeling weakened – it can calm fear, insecurity, hurt and anxiety. A smile can be good when we make a mistake – and we're just being 'stupidly human'; it can help us to brighten up and lighten up and not take everything too seriously.

# Motion And Emotion

Nature has assigned to human beings certain physical 'tells' that reveal the emotions that we're feeling at any given moment.

Every emotion that we experience, whether positive or negative, expresses itself through our bodies (outward display). There are so many windows that give exposure to these feelings. It could be through our facial expressions, the way we hold ourselves, the tone of our voice, the way we walk. You don't need to ask an angry person if they're angry, because the emotion will reveal itself: redness of the face, aggressively animated facial expressions, add to that a loud tone of voice, colourful language, exaggerated body movements and potentially excessive sweating.

Similarly, you don't need to ask a depressed person if they're depressed, as chances are, their posture will indicate the emotion, with slumped shoulders, eyes looking down, maybe with a look of hopelessness and helplessness on their face, and a monotone voice. They may walk in a slow, shuffling, uninspired and defeated way.

Also, you wouldn't need to ask a happy person if they were happy. Their posture would be erect, there would be a big smile on their face, there would be joyfully expressive gestures, great eye contact, deeper breathing, light-heartedness in their demeanour, and a spring in their step as they walk with power and purpose.

It's quite clear that the way you feel emotionally affects the way you feel physically, and the way you feel physically, affects the way you feel emotionally. It's the mind–body connection.

An experiment I often ask people to do is what I call 'The Power Groove'. I ask them to think about how they want to feel ... and then decide to take control and manifest that feeling by powering up their state by choosing and using powerful words to direct their thoughts; coupling this with exaggerated body language – animated gestures and facial expressions that are conducive to creating that feeling.

# "Be aware that your mindset is always on display through your face, voice and body."

© 2014 NJT

The objective is to raise energy by manifesting positive emotions – thus raising the vibration! You want to feel the vibes shimmering in your mind. You want to create a feeling of power and unstoppability.

The reports I receive back from people regarding this exercise are that the results are always positive and uplifting with a raised vibration and smiling faces.

There's no doubt that by deliberately using exaggerated movements and gestures we're much more able to manifest the feelings of confidence and power that we want, so really it's just a case of practising at every available opportunity.

# Appearance
## (Not The Best-Looking – But Looking My Best)

People look up to and admire those who are well-groomed – it can be a prerequisite to attractiveness and shows self-respect. It's important to look good (and appropriate) both at social events and in workday situations, because if you look good, chances are you'll feel good, which is essential for attracting and maintaining relationships and building your confidence and self-esteem.

Appropriate appearance is vital in any professional context. Sales professionals are expected to present themselves in a certain way to maximise the chances of making a sale. A pilot (and crew) would be expected to appear and behave in a certain way to win the confidence of their passengers and if you went to a surgeon who was likely to be operating on you, that person would be expected to behave appropriately to gain your trust and respect as their patient, but if they walked in with a cigarette, a glass of Scotch, slurring their words, there's every chance you might want to cancel that operation.

Enhancers of our appearance:

## Clothes

Firstly, clothes don't have to be boring in any situation, even if it's a formal business meeting. Men can add a touch of colour and interest with a handkerchief in their jacket breast pocket or by wearing a classy tie; women could add a scarf or some jewellery to reflect uniqueness and personality.

Your clothes should suit the occasion for which they're being worn. If it's a professional situation, they should be relevant to that environment. Going to a meeting wearing clothes that are so bold they appear to enter the room before you, and where they secure more attention than you do, is not going to win you much respect.

Clothes should always be clean and fresh and fit well. I remember having a boss once who always dressed in smartest tailored suits ... but I couldn't help from being distracted by the fact he would always tie his tie too short.

Your clothes are a visual calling card, communicating a message to people as loudly as, if not more than, what you say.

## Hair

Your hair style should fit and complement your personality, within reason, as well as the occasion – smart clothing will not be enhanced by hair that isn't well groomed, and an ordered appearance indicates that you're likely to have your life, career and world similarly thought out and in order.

## Nails

The condition of your nails can reveal a lot about you. If you have visible dirt beneath them, or they're ragged and untidy, it's likely to raise questions about your personal hygiene. Keep them well-maintained because they can play a big part in the overall impression you're endeavouring to make.

## Ladies' Make-Up

It should be used to stylishly enhance your overall impression. Generally, subtle is safer. Otherwise it may well end up having the opposite effect to the one desired. When it comes to perfume, don't overpower everyone; again, keep it subtle.

## Accessories

Too much bling ain't the thing! Any jewellery should be carefully selected to complement the overall impression that you're wishing to make, without being too distracting.

## Shoes

Clean up your act ... starting with your shoes! Your shoes should be quality, clean and appropriate for the occasion; and if they're fit for purpose it shows that you're paying attention to detail.

Don't leave your appearance undone! Banish the gum ... and always wear that smile...

Be yourself, and prosper!

# Breathe

Every breath you take is a vital elixir that plays an important part in your healthy lifestyle, energising your whole being and formulating your physiology.

Breathing shallowly can make us feel nervous, dull our mental abilities and cause harmful stress. I believe everyone should take the time to do some deep breathing exercises every day. When you flood your body with a full, oxygenated breath, you're allowing purity and energy to envelop your whole system, creating peace and serenity.

I believe the best method for deep breathing is the diaphragmatic method. The diaphragm is a dome-shaped muscle that sits horizontally across the base of the rib cage just below the lungs.

When you breathe in correctly it causes the diaphragm to contract and pull downwards and flatten. When you breathe out it returns to its normal resting position. By doing diaphragmatic breathing properly you can considerably decrease your chances of health problems.

I find this method more efficient when performed in a standing position.

Stand with shoulders relaxed.

Place one hand on your diaphragm and the other on your abdomen so you can 'feel' the procedure. Use the six-four-six method...

Breathe in deeply and steadily through the nose for a count of six, allowing the breath to flow in continuously and evenly with no pausing. If you're executing it correctly, you'll notice that your abdomen will move slightly but your upper chest will remain still. As you take the breath, visualise a life-enhancing power filling you to the brim. Hold for a count of four. Then as you exhale through the mouth for a count of six, see any fear, sorrow and frustration gently leaving your body. Breathe in deeply again, immediately.

Consider that during the course of a day you breathe in and out over twenty thousand times. With every breath you absorb around twenty millilitres of oxygen and dispose of a similar amount of carbon dioxide. If you take in a deep breath, a large shot of oxygen enters your circulatory system, and once there it joins forces with the red blood cells to produce energy for the removal of waste material. Shallow breaths, on the other hand, can fail to fulfil the body's oxygen requirements, with the result being that if you're feeling tense you may inadvertently tighten your muscles, constricting blood flow, which then raises your heart rate and stimulates stress hormones across the whole of your body, impairing the removal of waste products from the body and contributing to carbon dioxide and lactic acid building up in your muscle tissue.

In short, breathing intelligently guides your body to a place of calmness and tranquility (that's why it's so important in meditation), lowering your blood pressure and increasing your energy levels.

Make regular diaphragmatic breathing an essential part of your fitness regime.

# That Loving Feeling

A deep and beautiful loving relationship can do wonders for your health. Just hugging and holding hands can send a wave of happiness over your whole body. It's often the case that people who are in loving relationships feel the most content – having that strong emotional support is a definite booster for wellbeing.

We've all heard of the term 'sexual healing', made famous by a song of the same name – and it really is a health booster. Regular physical touch and sex can be incredibly beneficial for lowering blood pressure, exercising your heart and strengthening your immune system – it's great aerobic exercise, improving cardiovascular health, encouraging deep, restful sleep and stress reduction, burning calories and aiding weight loss, and contributing to a more youthful appearance with healthier skin tone, so boosting self-image and self-esteem.

Regular sex increases your levels of the 'love hormone' oxytocin, which encourages feelings of warmth, comfort and relaxation. It can even help relieve pain from headaches, migraines and arthritis.

Are you loved up?

# The Car Wash Story

I remember in my young days my dad saying to me, on more than one occasion, "Why don't you go and wash your car, it looks so dirty and dull?" At the time, like many youths, I wasn't very motivated and quite frankly, just couldn't be bothered ... and then, I met this gorgeous young girl: I fell madly in love with her and she fell madly in love with me. It was winter and we had unusually heavy snow that year, and my car disappeared in the white-out ... it looked more like an igloo than a car – just a white mound in the distance – no part of its red paint was visible ... and yet there I stood in my parents' outhouse with my bucket and sponge. My dad appeared – he stood there open-mouthed, "What are you doing?" "I'm going to wash my car," I replied enthusiastically. "Have you not looked out the window this morning?" "Yeah ... that won't stop me!" and off I went stomping through the snow towards my 'igloo'. Every stroke I made with that hot, soapy sponge was delivered with complete joy and freedom of spirit. There was no thought of it being a chore, no thought of 'couldn't be bothered', there was only purpose and pleasure and the heavy snow just added to the fun – I was in love, I was in lust and the current beneficiary was my car. As I lovingly washed away the dirt and dullness, the snow carried on falling as heavily as I can ever remember it doing, and I just about had time to admire my handiwork before, once again, it disappeared beneath the blanket of white. Oh the power of love!

# Meditation

Meditation can be amazingly beneficial when it comes to problem solving because it gives you clear access to your spiritual centre where all the answers to your every question can be sought. Important decisions can be made when you're in that serene place and your mind is in a calm objective state.

I believe the most beneficial time to practise meditation is before going to bed, especially if you've had a very stressful day, because to sleep properly we need to be in a relaxed state of mind.

The practice of meditation creates:

- That spiritual connection to your...
- Problem-solving hub, which is fundamental for...
- Emotional balance and...
- A fit, healthy mind and body.

The knock-on benefits are considerable:

- Reducing fatigue;
- Helping to clear headaches and migraines;
- Helping to lower high blood pressure;
- Aiding better sleep;
- Reducing the impact of worry, fear and stress.

When our emotional balance is positively directed it's effective in:

- Dissipating anger;
- Dissolving anxiety;
- Reducing depression;
- Eliminating negativity.

Meditating on gratitude gives you the chance to reclaim any power you may have inadvertently given away, by giving you the chance to re-centre and move away from negative focus and energise the positives that are in your life by redirecting your thoughts towards the things you want.

Use meditation as a tool from the PLB Code to help you attain the life you want by being part of that life right now – it's about habitual and continuous focus!! This means giving no thought or attention to anything that may nudge you off course.

Let's look at how we can begin meditation.

Many people have differing views on when and how to meditate and for how long. Some believe we should use gentle, soothing music as an audio backdrop for our journey within. Others are quick to tell us that we should meditate at a certain time of the day.

My personal view is that if you're just beginning, leave the music for another day and set some time aside during an evening. I believe evening meditation is preferable because the morning is a time when you've just come out of a sleeping cycle so your mind is not in need of more relaxation; if anything it's looking to be fired up for the day ahead. In the evening, however, you may be feeling the effects of a stressful and/or tiring day, and will benefit more from an opportunity to find calmness and serenity.

Ensure you have a five to ten minute time window when you know you're not going to be disturbed; find a suitable chair, turn off the light and get comfortable in your seated position with feet flat on the floor and your hands resting on your lap. Start to become aware of your breathing; all the time you're concentrating on your breath, your thoughts are directed away from any 'monkey chatter' that may be going on in your mind. It may take a while to silence that inner noise but with regular practice you'll notice it will gradually become easier to control. As you continue with your breathing awareness you'll notice calmness enveloping your body. If your mind starts to wander and the chattering returns, just concentrate, concentrate, concentrate on your breathing and once again any background distraction should dissipate.

As you become more and more comfortable with meditation you're likely to want to increase the time you spend practising, but the above-mentioned five to ten minutes is ideal to begin with.

There are many different ways of meditating, and I think it's something worth experimenting with to find the way which you find most suitable and effective for you.

# Massage

Massage delivered by the human touch – is there a more pleasurable way of helping us feel calm, joyous and totally connected?

By rubbing and kneading parts of the body for relief and for pleasure, easing away stress and tension from our muscles and our minds we help ourselves to relax, lowering our blood pressure, improving our circulation, our flexibility and our immune system. Massage also helps us combat the unpleasant effects of headaches, migraines and eye strain, making it an indispensable part of our health regime.

There are many types of massage that are worth experimenting with but the one I want to share with you in this book is my personal favourite: the head massage.

I'd recommend creating an enticing environment to complement the experience, using scented candles, having soft lighting and playing relaxing music. Allow fifteen to twenty minutes for this massage.

My favourite type of head massage involves using oil; there are many different types of scented massage oil readily available from high street stores, but you can also use any of the following which you may already have in one of your cupboards: coconut oil, sesame oil, virgin olive oil or palm oil.

If you're the masseur/masseuse, ask your recipient to remove any neck jewellery and to sit upright in a comfortable chair. Stand behind them and begin smoothing their hair by running your hands over the top of it in long sweeping strokes, before running your fingers through it from top to bottom – this will remove any tangles. Pour a small amount of oil into the palm of your hand, rub your hands together to cover them evenly and then apply to the hair with the same stroking motion – once again from top to bottom. Use the tips of your fingers to facilitate even distribution, and lightly massage into their scalp.

When the first application of oil is complete, repeat the procedure to further cover the hair and scalp. If the hair is quite long, lift it up from the ends and run your fingers upwards through it from underneath – reach all areas around the hairline including the sides and front, running your fingers upwards at the sides massaging the scalp as you go.

Now make the third and final application of oil making sure all areas are covered. Use your fingers to comb through the hair, keeping movements nice and light. You can now try finger circles down the middle of the head and then down the sides of the hairline starting at the temples, once again from top to bottom and nice and slow. Follow this with gentle hair pulls, twists and tugs and soft plucks. Apply static finger pressure at various places over the scalp to stimulate the nerve endings, then place the hands into the hair at the sides of the head and slowly bring the hands together interlocking the fingers and gently squeezing the scalp. Repeat from front to back.

A fabulous way to finish is to move onto the face. Try some gentle strokes across the forehead from the middle outwards – follow this by making circles around the eyes in opposite directions, then pull softly on the eyebrows. Move on to the centre of the chin and make gentle finger circles along the length of the jawbone; then, the same finger circles on the temples, and finish off by kneading and pulling on the ears.

Leaving the oil in the hair for an hour or so is a great way to condition the hair and scalp, and it's easy to shampoo out at the end.

The recipient should now feel an amazing sense of calm and positive wellbeing and any tensions or anxieties, any headaches, migraines or eye strain should completely melt away. Of all the massage techniques out there I would most recommend the head massage ... in fact, I would say that it's one of the most highly effective stress-busters available.

# Sleep

Adequate sleep is crucial if we're to function at our best, and be alert, dynamic and energised, productive and cognitively sharp.

It's not only the amount of sleep that's important; the quality of our sleep is equally vital, because being properly rested helps us to concentrate, analyse, remember, make important decisions, and generally be much more effective in all our undertakings. It's also a major determinant in our longevity.

Sleep deprivation can set us on a downward spiral affecting our minds and our bodies. It can aggravate diabetes and contribute to heart disease, and suppress and compromise our immune systems – making us more susceptible to illness and infection. If your defences are low and your immune systems' power degraded, it will be unable to do its job properly.

A compromised immunity can lead to an inflammatory response in the blood vessels and arteries in our cardiovascular system which can lead to strokes and heart attacks. It has also been proven that a lack of sleep can slow your body's response to vaccines and slow the creation of antibodies needed to fight disease. Sleep alone won't prevent you from becoming sick, but it can definitely help in reducing the likelihood of sickness occurring, and its severity if it does.

We all know too well how a lack of sleep can cause us to feel cranky, run-down and fatigued, exacerbating symptoms such as anxiety, depression, paranoia, irritability and anger, and can have an effect on your mental functioning, including your memory – for example, your responses may be slower, which, if you're driving, could have dangerous consequences, in fact, it may even make you as slow at responding as a drunk driver.

Sleep is restorative. It heals the body, clears and quietens the mind and restores balance to the soul. Deep sleep is a welcome retreat from the 'noise' of the outside world – it gives time for being rather than doing.

# Artificial Stimulants

It's hard to quantify the destructive effect drugs can have in every area of your life, from your own mental and physical well-being to the wider effect on family and friends. Complete avoidance really is the only way to go here. I personally realised as a young person that drug-taking was a line that must never be crossed.

It's quite clear that people who are happy and positive have no need for these artificial stimulants. They already feel high on life and enthusiastic about the future because they've made the decision to live smart and intelligently, and it would be an unintelligent decision to voluntarily allow smoke, drugs or excessive alcohol to enter our systems. It's a fact that the more positive we are the easier it is to handle the stresses and strains that come our way. By taking the events of our lives in our stride, we can observe and correct, any time that we start to wobble and lose our balance-awareness.

# Smoking

Well here it is – my pet peeve – smoking! So what's my problem? In my opinion this is, without exception, the biggest waste of time known to man. It's a loser's habit!! Does this mean that if you're a smoker you're a loser? No, it doesn't. Let me explain – what I'm saying is that all the time you're smoking, you're losing...

Let's look a little closer at how:

- It's a major cause of lung cancer and heart disease.

- It's a major contributor to bronchitis and emphysema.

- It smells disgusting.

- It stains your teeth, fingers, etc.

- It's anti-social.

- It gives you bad breath.

- It causes your senses of taste and smell to become impaired.

- It makes you cough.

- It can make you less fertile.

- It can make your skin look older.

- It will lower your energy level.

- It suppresses your immune system – more colds and flu!

- It costs you money!!

...and all of this for something that you don't need ... being a smoker is not living intelligently, it's not living smart and completely goes against the principles of the PLB Code.

I must admit, I'm a big believer in the American 'cold turkey' approach to giving up this pointless habit. Cutting down is not the answer – because if you do that you're still moving in the wrong direction ... just more slowly. Let me ask you a straight question: "What are the benefits of smoking?" Don't go quiet on me now.

I think you know the answer – there aren't any, so if you're losing by being a smoker ... you can become a winner as soon as you quit, therefore make that decision ... NOW! If you were told that if you didn't stop your thirty-a-day habit by this time next week, you'd be dead, believe me you'd stop, so I urge you to take it that seriously and remove this big negative from your life, and receive positives from all five of the PLB areas at the same time.

a)   **Mental Fitness area** – clearer thinking – more alert.

b)   **Physical Fitness area** – feel more energised – less breathlessness.

c)   **Relationship Fitness area** – more socially acceptable – more friends.

d)   **Financial Fitness area** – this one is obvious!

e)   **Fun Fitness area** – less restricted in what you do – more freedom.

If you don't want to end up as a statistic – then this habit needs to go. Break the habit before it breaks you.


# Physical Fitness Action Invitation

Below are vital ingredients that when added to all the other ingredients in the PLB Code mixing bowl, and worked on consistently, will lead you towards being the excuse-free success you've always wanted to be. It's about creating daily disciplines of action to create momentum.

Decide to:

- Make exercise a regular part of your health regime – it shows respect for your body; your vehicle of life.

- Take nutrition seriously by selecting some of my suggested top 20 superfoods to be included in your diet.

- Work on your body language so that the first impressions you make are always positive.

- Always look your best – your appearance is vital to how you're perceived by others.

- Use deep diaphragmatic breathing as a vital health elixir – flooding your whole system with life-promoting oxygen.

- Use meditation to connect to your spiritual hub and disconnect from the daily noise.

- Experiment with the many different types of massage – it can be great fun and an enjoyable way of relieving tension.

- Make-love regularly. It gives your whole body a great work-out – it's good for your heart and good for your mind.

- Get adequate restorative sleep – it helps you stay mentally and physically sharp.

- Drop the bad stuff – the smoking, the over consumption of alcohol and any drug use.

# Chapter 4

## THE PLB CODE

# RELATIONSHIP FITNESS

**THE STUDENT**

# Relationships

**Relationships are all about your state of connectedness to other people and the environment, but often, with today's high-speed, high-pressure busy, busy lifestyles, we may lose that connection because we're so totally consumed by our own lives, so much so that often we don't even give ourselves time to notice our environment or even to greet our neighbours.**

Usually, the first relationship experience we have is with our parents who have the first effect on our emotional development, which asserts an influence that can stay with us on a subconscious level for a lifetime.

Often, people who have had the good fortune to have been brought up in a close, loving family will feel much more emotionally secure than those whose upbringing has been more turbulent and troubled – maybe parental separation, or even divorce, can lead them to feeling unloved and abandoned.

Outside of the family, we begin to develop relationships with other people: in pre-school groups and then in school itself, at social events as we become young adults and then eventually in the workplace and the broader society. In all these environments, we meet people who have different personalities and beliefs to us and some may prove challenging to be around and to work with. Some will remain acquaintances, some will become our friends. Some may even become our lovers, and spouses.

As we grow in confidence, experience and maturity, we're much more able to handle any difficult situations that arise, and with an innate belief in our own capabilities we're more likely to progress to bigger challenges where if we gain the trust and respect of our colleagues for our ability to successfully manage others, so they feel 'safe in our hands', this can lead us to being effective in team building and fostering business relationships.

Ultimately, life is one long series of differing connections and the more open and skilful we become at managing those connections the more rewarding our journey through life is likely to be.

# Friendship

The starting point for friendship has to be the relationship you have with yourself ... being your own best friend. Usually, those who have a caring, accepting, 'happy in their own skin' attitude towards themselves radiate a loving energy that's there for all to see ... but more about that in a moment.

It's true what they say that we teach others how to treat us by the way we treat ourselves, and this goes back to our self-image as discussed in the Mental Fitness chapter. The better we feel about ourselves the more likely we're to build quality friendships with others and what an amazing life-enhancer that can be – so valuable, so priceless! These special connections can lift your spirits when you're feeling down, put a smile on your face, show you that you're loved and give you hope.

What an unusual and mysterious social process friendship is though. Some say that we seek friends who display similar traits to ourselves – but often this is not the case. I believe we select friends on a subconscious level, with a myriad of different reasons influencing our decision making process: whether we perceive them to be trustworthy or not, whether we find them fun, physically attractive or kind and non-threatening.

It's clear that in many situations people will choose friends that are of a similar age, social status, education or profession. Academic people will usually have academic friends, religious people religious friends. Musicians will often hang out with other musicians and so it goes on.

All friendships need to be worked at to keep them alive – some won't go the distance; and it can be better to let them go. Others may nourish you to your very core; comfort you, encourage you, help you grow and bloom ... and they're the ones we want more of. They're the true friends who are genuine, and always there for you when you need them – they help you to relax and feel comfortable and secure in yourself. You share with them a bond of trust which means anything private remains that way.

You always know where you stand with your real friends; they're solid as a rock. That doesn't mean they'll agree with everything you say, but will value your friendship high enough to not allow any minor differences of opinion to get out of hand.

How can we widen our circle of friends?

First make peace with yourself, as mentioned above, by increasing your self-love and self-respect, and then, when you meet new people, show an interest in them and their lives, minimise the use of the 'I' word. Celebrate their victories not just your own. Always be open to who your friends can be – have friends who are from a different age group, friends who are from a different culture or social class, because the reality is, even though we're all different, we're all very much the same. In other words, we may come from completely diverse backgrounds, but we all want to live a happy life, do the best for our families, and to be as successful and as fulfilled in our own lives as we possibly can, so smile and make good eye contact, be upbeat in your mood – display that 'great to be alive' feeling. People are attracted to those who radiate warmth and positivity, so never gossip about anyone or become involved in negative conversations, instead be kind, helpful and interested, and more than likely, you'll find yourself in demand with a strong network of great friends.

# Our Relationship With Ourselves

Let's come back to our relationship with ourselves. It all comes down to our self-image and self-esteem as discussed in the Mental Fitness chapter, because this, in a nutshell, is what controls our behaviour.

It's clear that our relationship with ourselves is based on our conditioning through our life experiences – positive and negative – that have found their way into our subconscious mind. We have an inbuilt system that filters everything we have experienced through our senses that gives us a result that reflects our history ... and results in us often becoming a product of those experiences – our values and beliefs generally being informed by them if not formed as a result of them. Our memories aren't always 100% accurate, though, but may appear that way to us due to these filters. For example, you stare out the window at the pouring rain and you feel a little depressed because you have interpreted it as being somewhat miserable, and unpleasant. Another person could look out at the same scene and see it as being refreshing, cleansing and delightful – helping all the plants to grow.

Whichever your response, it's neither right nor wrong – it's simply your conditioning which will determine your interpretation of the event.

It's definitely possible to change the relationship we have with ourselves – it just takes effort and a will to succeed. The unhelpful and outdated patterns of behaviour that we've developed over time need to be identified and replaced, with the replacements energising us to move in a life-enhancing direction.

The more that we can build our own relationship the more positive knock-on effects there will be for our relationships with others.

When you know that you have a special relationship with yourself you feel free to move in the direction you want to go because you'll have a high degree of self-trust – you know you can count on yourself to get the job done. Your self-image will be strong, your self-esteem will be healthy and you'll have a clear sense of purpose. Also, you'll genuinely like yourself and be accepting of your faults and foibles.

It's such an inspired way to live your life because if you constantly need others' verification for your self-worth – craving praise and approval – this can become like a thirst that forever needs quenching, and if you don't receive that verification, you may suffer from, what I call 'dehydration of self-love', which means your confidence and self-esteem are compromised – they dry up, and this can be very destructive.

I personally find it fun and challenging to work at anything that enhances my wellbeing; replacing learnt destructive patterns of behaviour with growth-promoting ones is well worth the initial work involved to make them a permanent part of my psyche.

Try it. You won't look back.

# Eleven Pillars Of A Strong Personal Relationship

Relationships need to be reciprocal. A relationship that leans more towards one partner than the other is one which is out of balance, and not offering the opportunity for the two to grow and flourish together. Thoughts, feelings and emotions need to be shared so both parties feel significant and valued. The following are eleven ways in which we can maximise our chances of success.

# Respect

It's often said that you should treat people in the way you would like to be treated yourself. A healthy mutual respect can be a good foundation for any relationship to be built on. So what is respect and why is it so important? It's a combination of admiration for, acceptance and recognition of a person and their perceived worth. Taking time to fully listen to what the other person has to say; the giving of your time and undivided attention shows respect for the other party and will most certainly increase their respect for you. Some people believe you can earn respect through fear and intimidation, but it's not about ruling by fear ... you can't force respect! True respect is when you can look at someone and recognise qualities in them which are 'respect earners'. Often it's the way they carry themselves, the way they behave, the standards they adhere to. They appear happy in themselves and come across as confident, competent and out-going.

# Honesty

Being honest with people is usually the best policy, even when the truth can hurt. If you can be honest but kind, honest but tactful, honest but considerate, the chances are no real damage will be done. Your word reflects your integrity, and it can be healthy for a relationship if people are always clear where they stand – so lay things on the table, open up and be transparent.

When you lie, you challenge your own integrity, and you weaken your standing in the eyes of the other person(s). Also, telling lies can be difficult to keep up with and you may end up getting caught out, as trying to remember what you said and when you said it just leads to confusion and conflict.

Working through any points of contention in any situation with honesty and maturity is without doubt the best success-generating route you can take.

## Acceptance

It's easier to accept someone if we can first be accepting of ourselves. If we can accept our own unique quirks and ways of being, then accepting someone else's can be that much easier. Often, we don't like traits that others have because they can mirror those that we dislike in ourselves. Equally, we may become irritated by someone because they're displaying a behaviour trait that we wish we had. Also, we may find someone else's behaviour might actually not be compatible with or challenge our values, which, if we don't keep our control, can lead us to anger.

Accepting someone doesn't mean you have to agree with everything they say and do – acknowledging them for who they are without trying to change them is half the battle. Often, areas of disagreement can be beneficial in promoting a strong and dynamic relationship. It's important when disagreement occurs that the discord is handled with maturity, and not allowed to develop into anything more. Your relationship can flourish when you're accepting of each other's position even if you don't agree.

## Compromise

This is all about creating win-win situations, and behaving in a way that allows the other party to feel that they're important and have been listened to, treated fairly and shown respect. Without compromise (the universal peacemaker), your integrity with regards your relationship could be challenged and strained.

Some people see compromising as a sign of weakness – but in fact, if anything it shows maturity and recognition of another person's rights and feelings; it shows goodwill to all those involved. The only time it could be seen as a weakness is if you feel you're being manipulated or taken advantage of, and you don't act to rectify this.

# Appreciation

Appreciation is a great way to express love and caring. Showing appreciation for someone demonstrates to them how much you value them, and your relationship with them. Show through both your actions and your words and your relationship will go from strength to strength. Not everyone finds it easy to demonstrate how they feel – "it goes without saying (or showing)" being a familiar turn of phrase – but a little bit of effort goes a long way. Otherwise, you may open doors to unintended emotional turmoil where your partner becomes unsure of where they stand with you, so let them know when you appreciate a thought, word or action, and do something in return that shows how much you care ... give a smile, give a gift, give their spirit a lift ... and your relationship will flourish.

# Trust

Trust is the back-bone to any healthy relationship; it's the cement between the bricks which comprise your partnership's walls. It's an amazing and special gift when you can share your feelings and emotions with someone else and have a faith in their honesty, integrity and credibility. If that trust is broken, though, it can mean the end of the relationship, as doubt and uncertainty rear their ugly heads, as walls where the cement has been allowed to crack and crumble will become unstable and may even come crashing down.

Be the trust as you seek the trust and your relationship will stand with solid walls.

# Personal Space

Personal space is such a valuable ingredient in the longevity of a relationship. Everyone needs time to themselves, time to do their own thing ... time out!

Many a good relationship comprises building blocks of togetherness, companionship and intimacy; however, after time, too much togetherness can lead to a relationship that's suffocating and stifling, creating tension and boredom.

It's a natural thing that people need personal space sometimes – it's not personal towards the other partner, it's just the way we're wired. Your partner may have some interests you don't like, for example, or even some friends, that you don't get along with, but instead of trying to stop them pursuing those interests or seeing those friends, you should give them space and accept their boundaries. Show them that you respect and trust them. There's no need for them to give up everything from their old single life, especially if it's something that they love doing – and the same applies to you. If both parties in a relationship encourage, motivate and support each other in all that they do, the partnership is more likely to flourish and bloom and be healthy and meaningful.

# Humour

Humour can bring joy and appreciation to a relationship, adding interest and excitement. A relationship which involves laughter and fun can be incredibly beneficial to its longevity as it keeps the spark alive. Being playful with your partner can help initiate the feel-good factor and prolong the harmony; it gives it a real glow and a flow.

Humour can be great for relieving stress. If you've had a bad day and you feel irritable and argumentative, humour can help diffuse tension before things get out of hand, with someone saying something they later wished they hadn't.

Humour is a great way to connect. Humour is sexy, smiling is sexy and enjoying your life is sexy! It's an attractive personality trait and medicine for your spirit. It's infectious! Make humour a compulsory part of your relationship.

## Clear Communication

This is a key component in any healthy relationship. Being clear with regards where you both stand and where you're going with your relationship leaves no room for misunderstanding and confusion, and is an open and honest way to proceed.

How foolish it is to go days feeling hurt by and upset with your partner or them with you, because of some insensitive and misplaced remarks, when a little thought and clear communication would have avoided the involvement of troublesome emotions.

By communicating openly and tactfully, by listening and not blaming, we can avoid any hurt and can actively promote happy feelings, free of anxiety and misunderstandings, where trust is maintained and a successful resolution to any issues is more likely.

## Commitment

When you choose to spend a large amount of your precious time with another person and to show them unconditional love, this can reasonably be seen as the ultimate commitment – it's an agreement to learn together and grow together.

There will surely be times when the road becomes rocky and the seas stormy, but if the commitment is built on strong legs of loyalty it can overcome any obstacles that dare cast shadows on its path. Spending time together, resisting temptation and supporting each other through good and bad – these are the staples of a great relationship.

## Forgiveness

We're all fallible, we all make mistakes, saying the wrong things at the wrong time ... sometimes appearing to be totally uncaring and insensitive ... acting before engaging our brains. We forget important anniversaries or to make calls we promised. It isn't necessarily intentional; it's just that we're human and often have too many things going on such that we forget through our own preoccupation.

It's important that we can forgive even though we may not forget, and not allow something that, in the grand scheme of things, really isn't that important and is too trivial to be a key factor in the ruination of a great relationship.

**Common interests can be the key to a great relationship.**

# Love

Love – that most magical of human emotions. Our lives are embellished with songs of love that make our hearts sing, of films that make our eyes moist ... of feelings that are stirred and give us a warm glow on the inside on the coldest night. It's a subject that we never grow tired of. A story of when two hearts meet.

We've been widely advised to give love to one another – to spread love all around. Sceptics, always looking for a rational explanation, may see it as being no more than a human-invented chemical process going on in the brain, whereas those of a more romantic nature may see it as being part of a divine process where we're put here on this planet to connect with that special soulmate.

Whatever the reality, we would certainly be poorer for its absence.

Love is about caring, sharing, giving ... of being. It offers a higher vibration where the world looks clearer and happier and more welcoming. Don't be blinded by its brightness, though, as on some occasions it could be an illusion; the devil disguised as a dove, robbing you of your dignity ... and possessions. We must always be aware of its benefits and hidden dangers. Many a strong man has been brought to his knees and reduced to a pitiful state by an unrequited love. Many a 'thunderous tyrant' has been reduced to the level of an obedient puppy by the love of a special woman.

When it's for real, though, it carries a magic like no other. Sometimes it can be worth jumping through the flaming hoops, running across the burning coals, just to bathe in its glory. It can be the key element that sees someone come through adversity and rise above defeat. It has a power all of its own.

Really, love is omnipotent, featuring prominently in all five PLB Code areas: bringing sunshine into our lives, putting a spring in our step and creating an air of fun, fun, fun. Love the love!

# Our Relationship With The Environment

When we talk about our relationship with the environment, what this really involves is the realisation and understanding that even though Planet Earth is a remarkable place, a gift to us all that should be respected, we're trapped here; unable to leave and expand to other domains, due to the vast distances of space and unprecedented levels of radiation that exist outside of Earth's atmosphere. Maybe one day in the far distant future, mankind will be able to travel to, explore and settle on other planets, but for now and the long foreseeable future we must make the most of what we have.

Everything we have comes from the environment of our small planet: the air we breathe, the food we eat, the water we drink, the clothes we wear... everything! It all comes from our priceless and precious jewel of life.

Mankind, being the dominant species, has the responsibility, as guardians of this small but wonderfully made dot in the cosmos. We're entrusted to oversee that the planet remains strong, vibrant and life-sustaining for future generations not only of people but of all animal and plant species too, so they too can enjoy all its amazing benefits and not inherit a dying, sterile domain. We're the gardeners; we're the farmers who must preserve the dynamic balance of our precious jewel's landscape. There's no future if we choose to govern without respect.

I believe there's a gradual shift taking place in the collective human consciousness, resulting in an ever-increasing drive towards global harmony. There's recognition that all creatures and all plants have a right to their place on this planet, and the more this awareness increases, the more efforts will be made to protect the oceans from being used like a giant open sewer, and the planet's precious, finite resources from being exploited to exhaustion. More rational thinking will mean greater understanding of and more direct action towards preserving the forests, reducing pollutants, increasing recycling and generally more proactive housekeeping.

I don't agree with the critics, the naysayers and the prophets of doom who say that we're in an unstoppable free-fall towards inevitable destruction. I believe that we as a species are better than that – we have the power to recognise when things are starting to lose their alignment and are able to initiate rapid action for the return of equilibrium.

All major crises lead to changes in attitudes, changes in understanding, and changes in behaviour as we step forward to re-establish the relationship of trust and respect with our planet. We need to recognise that we're all in this together and must play our part in actions and deeds, not just words.

As we renew this alliance with our environment we will need to initiate worldwide discussion and co-operation to create a future framework that addresses issues such as, for example, population growth, and the preservation of the natural habitat. I do believe the day will come when certain parts of the world will be designated as protected areas; and administered by the global community, for the benefit of the planet and all its living things, and not 'owned' by a single or a few countries; I would cite the Amazon and the Congo as two possible examples. Also, through necessity, global answers will have to be found – through education and discussion – to the issue of population increase ... I'm sure the future will bring controls and even the 'encouraged' migration of people to less populated areas of the world as they become more developed and life-sustaining, Australia, for example and the Sahara in Africa. Of course, there will always be those who care not for their fellow man or for the planet and who happily wallow in overconsumption and selfish greed, but I do believe the collective will of the majority will win through in the end.

As time goes on we're growing as a species, moving on to a new stage; we're leaving behind the old mindsets where people were devalued and prejudged against the colour of their skin, their religion, their sexual preferences, their abilities and disabilities or their degree of wealth.

# "Life's too short to be racist."

© 2014 NJT

Society is beginning to mature and to acknowledge the importance of being about more than just face value. Age-old suspicions are being put to one side as people develop a greater respect and understanding for those who may not be like them. If we can all guide our breath in this positive direction then the future doesn't need to be seen as a frightening and dark place, but instead as a bright land of hope and harmony.

## Those Who Surround Us

Every one of us is susceptible to the influence of the people who are part of our lives. Beware of those who take advantage; beware of those who may impact you negatively, whether emotionally, physically or financially. For example, if you spend a lot of time with people who habitually spend all their money and are permanently broke; living from one pay day to the next, take care that you don't absorb their negative habits.

Beware of telling the wrong people of your hopes and plans for the future, as they'll be standing ready to trash your dreams with the glee of a child kicking over another child's sandcastles. Beware the 'chippers' and dream-stealers who are constantly attacking your aspirations, gently nudging you off course, clipping your wings to stop you soaring like an eagle, and undermining your confidence so that your positive focus becomes increasingly blurred. It then becomes harder and harder for you to raise the energy to escape their clutches. You may even end up becoming one of them! Beware of the people who aggravate misfortune by constantly complaining about the weather, the government, their bad luck ... everything. Their disease could be contagious.

Misery loves company and these people want to make you a part of theirs and keep you at their level. That's their agenda, it's not yours. We all, from time to time, come into contact with these kinds of people. They're poison to your positive attitude, they want to throw water on your fire of life, and they're the force that will guarantee to wipe the smile from your face with their negative griping. They have much pain in their lives ... most of it imagined ... and they want to share it with you.

Sometimes negative people can take you unawares. It can be a surprise attack, a rain shower of verbal acid. The poisonous cloud that they emit can be all-enveloping and it can be difficult to avoid breathing in some of their toxic emissions ... but it can be done! With determination you can avoid their harmful vapours and so not be contaminated. If the toxic person is close to you – a long-time friend or a family member perhaps, then this may create a delicate situation where you have to make an assertive choice to spend less time with them, or work more on your own positive strategies to lessen their impact ... maybe even introduce them to the PLB Code. Now, don't get me wrong, I'm not advocating that if you have a loved one who may be facing serious problems of one kind or another, and needs your help, that you should banish them from your life. I'm talking about those who have it all and yet are still whining and griping.

With your PLB Code-generated powerful, positive, success-oriented attitude you may be somewhat mystified by their constant gloom ... but their behaviour can still leave you a little downcast. Just remember that they want to share the contents of their mental dustbin ... with you! The audacity of them! – To think that you would have the slightest interest in sifting through their rubbish with them. You must educate them, and fast! Disregarding their comments can be the first step; removing yourself from their company as quickly as possible could be the second. Don't think about them, don't talk about them – become a 'professional ignorer'; declare them irrelevant – that you don't rate them or their opinions.

Once you've distanced yourself from their toxic fumes you'll need to immediately refocus on the positive, success-directing life force that flows within you ... you'll soon be back to your charming, enthusiastic self!

You need to spend your life surrounded by people who genuinely support you, people who are fired up about their own life, and yours! These are the people you should be with.

**Embrace** the people who speak of victories, not defeats; hope not despair.

**Embrace** the people who see beauty in the rain, the soil ... in everyone and everything.

**Embrace** the people who are truly alive, who take joy from every corner of life.

**Embrace** the people who care not about colour, creed or sexual preference but see everyone as being part of the family that is humanity.

**Embrace** the people who embrace you and feed your self-esteem with words of encouragement. These people are the ones who you want in your life: positive, like yourself; they're the ones who appreciate the sunshine. Their personalities shower you with light and warmth, they talk of the good things in life, they give hope and strength and have the wisdom to be in tune with the reality that 'this is it' – this is your life and the game is on now, it's not a dress rehearsal, or as the Americans would say: there's no do-over!

Always remember that you have more power than you think!

# The Toxic Business Meeting

A number of years ago I attended a business meeting. At this meeting I was expecting to speak to a professional adviser who would give me some valuable tips on how to proceed with an idea I'd had. I wanted to hire a small, local theatre and perform a trial stage show combining music I'd written with humorous banter and my love of personal development.

The week before the meeting I was asked to supply details, so that the adviser would know in advance which areas I needed guidance in, and so would be in a better position to help me.

When I met this man, it was clear that he'd found my idea amusing ... he'd even brought along a colleague to sit in on what was about to become a farce of a business meeting. He proceeded to ask me questions about my plans while his colleague (pet monkey) sat at the side of the room giggling. I realised that instead of a positive, productive meeting, this was no more than him taking the opportunity to ridicule me and my idea. He assured me that, "professional business people would laugh this idea out the door," and then followed this up by saying, "Have you got funding for this project?" Before I had a chance to answer he took out his wallet and said with a smirk, "Neil, I really want to help you with this venture, so here's some money." He pulled out a £20 note and pretended to hand it to me before snatching it back and joining his colleague in fits of laughter. He then glanced at his notes, saw that I was a member of Toastmasters International and then proceeded to tell me what nonsense it was to stand up after dinner in a red coat to deliver a toast. By this time I'd lost all interest and decided against correcting his ignorance. The meeting ended with him returning to my idea and saying, "Neil, leave it alone." How about that for toxic people; how about that for professional business advisers?

He gave me a form that I was supposed to fill in, stating whether I'd found the business meeting helpful etc. I never did send it back to the company that had organised the meeting but instead kept it as a reminder that you should never allow toxic people to control your destiny.

Less than two years after this event, I performed my first successful solo show at a packed local theatre, featuring my music, humorous banter and personal development ... and that's what I do to this day.

# The Toxic Work Colleague

I once worked for a large company where there was a particular young individual who was continually criticising and condemning everyone else – undermining the positions of many senior staff (including me), some more than double his age. I found this guy totally disrespectful and thought that his attitude lacked any kind of integrity. Many of the senior staff had treated him kindly and helpfully only to be betrayed by his constant criticism behind their backs.

The manager, who wasn't always present in the department, had no reason to disbelieve this individual, when he 'sold himself up' by knocking everyone else down; trying to make his colleagues look small so he would look more capable and better qualified. His downfall came when the manager, taken in by this apparently super-confident individual, unexpectedly promoted him to a much more responsible and senior position ... to the surprise even of the individual himself.

Obviously, his super-confidence was more fragile than we thought ... he finally lost his bravado a week or so before he was due to start his new position and left the company. I and everyone else were ecstatic!

With the speed of his exit from the company his true colours were at last being shown. It didn't take long for everyone to realise that it was his lack of confidence that was making him behave the way he was. If this guy felt that he could only win promotion by deflating and devaluing his work colleagues rather than having faith in his own abilities and showing them off – then that's sad! Unless he changes his attitude and learns a few people skills, and starts working towards getting along with others rather than alienating them – he's very likely to remain one of life's losers.

I'm sure this story sounds familiar to a lot of people ... and handling a situation like this can be very difficult.

I was being undermined as much as anyone else but I refused to react. Yes, I found him discourteous but I retained the power over my own mind. It would have been too easy to have been made to want to leave the company and get another job, because most of us there were, at the time, happy in the jobs we were doing and didn't want to leave.

There were some colleagues who were quite affected by his behaviour and were worried that their own future promotion opportunities would be at risk. "When someone's been throwing dirt, some of it sticks!" was one the comments I often heard, but it was really a case of seeing the situation differently ... about realising that this individual 'owns his own behaviour' and that you own yours – it's that power of choice again ... choosing positive responses. This guy has as much power over you as you allow him, so in real terms, NONE!

In this situation practising the strategies of the PLB Code will allow you to extinguish the fire before it has a chance to catch hold.

# Relationship Fitness Action Invitation

Below are vital ingredients that when added to all the other ingredients in the PLB Code mixing bowl, and worked on consistently, will lead you towards being the excuse-free success you've always wanted to be. It's about creating daily disciplines of action to create momentum.

Decide to:

- Approach all your relationships from a positive perspective.

- If you have great family members, never miss an opportunity to let them know how important they are to you.

- Nurture your most valued friendships – for they're priceless.

- Love much – circulate it widely and give it generously.

- Remove yourself as quickly as possible from the company of those who are not for you.

- Maintain a respectful relationship with the environment – life's a flower garden.

- Maintain a healthy and loving relationship with yourself at all times – use the insights you've gained from the Mental Fitness chapter to keep your self-esteem in tip-top condition.

- Familiarise yourself with the "Eleven Pillars Of A Strong Personal Relationship" on **page 141** – and apply them to your own relationship, and if you don't have one at the moment, it will give you a greater understanding for when you do.

- Embrace those who speak of victories and success and who appreciate and respect you.

# Chapter 5

# FINANCIAL FITNESS

# Abundance

**How do you feel when money is tight? Do you feel restricted and compressed as if you're living your life trapped in a box with no escape? Do you feel as if your hands are tied behind your back or you're in a straitjacket and can hardly move? Do you feel overwhelmed and frustrated at not being able to do the things that you'd really like to do?**

What you're experiencing in your outer world is a reflection of what you're experiencing in your inner world, so if your conditioning is showing you lack and scarcity on the inside, then your outer reality will present the same. The Financial Fitness area teaches us the importance of working at switching our focus away from the financial limitations and restrictions in our lives and towards possibilities and opportunities. If you're worrying about not having enough to pay your bills, for example, or feeling frustrated because you can't afford to do the things you want to and you're starting to feel resentment towards people who are doing much better than you, then it's time you started practising redirecting your focus towards creating a wealthier mindset. We know that it's not easy to focus on the positive when we're experiencing great difficulties and challenges – it can be hard to move away from fear, anxiety and frustration and focus on abundance and success. You can try so hard, but when you're consumed by your problems the negatives are unbelievably persistent and keep coming back time and time again.

Use every tool available in the PLB Code to raise your vibration and re-establish your personal power – attack the unproductive mindset on many fronts – the road to success is paved with small victories. Use meditation, practise deep breathing, do some vigorous exercise, and spend some quiet time just working on positively redirecting those thoughts. Consult with people you trust and brainstorm ways of managing your finances as efficiently as possible.

Anything worth doing is worth doing badly to start with – just as long as you begin. Practise tuning into abundance from an internal perspective until you can manifest it on the outside – use your imagination to see it, hear it, smell it, touch it and feel it. You might find doing this is quite easy and routine. For those who have a greater resistance to allowing the natural flow, however, and who feel that they've already tried so many times without any tangible results, may find they've been trying too hard and have become consumed with the struggle, and are so overwhelmed with the task that they give up out of pure exhaustion. All abundance should be about ease and flow, so don't get anxious and fall prey to impatience, which is all too easy to do. Being in too much of a hurry with the 'I want it now' attitude is likely to repel rather than attract, making your intention tense and stress-filled, and as a result your vibration will be low, and you'll then, only attract more of the same.

Often, when you feel you've had enough, when you're feeling sick and tired of being sick and tired, is when you finally 'let go and let flow' and release all resistance, and this is when a shift occurs and you start to see progress take place, albeit small. Maybe this would be a good time to look closely at your relationship with money. Do you see it as scarce; where you never have enough to get by and can't see any possible way of getting any more? Do you feel envious of people who seem to have abundance flowing towards them with seemingly effortless ease? These are signs that your relationship with money needs work. At this point I would suggest that you bookmark this page, and turn to my three-way approach to handling money – "The PPF Formula" on **page 176.** Use this as a simple first step strategy to begin changing your financial relationship. The bigger goal would be for you to get to a place where you feel completely comfortable with money: the amount you have, that you can attract more, that some people have more than you. To get to this place takes effort – consistent effort – with the PPF formula the starting point.

Let's focus on some empowering thoughts to kick things off. Does having plenty of money make you feel excited, happy, expressive and free? If it does, hold that thought – doesn't it feel good when you can feel the rope that has bound your hands behind your back being cut, the box you've been trapped in being opened, and you being released from the straightjacket that has restricted you for so long?

Take every opportunity to practise thinking of being more affluent, and being free to do whatever activities you enjoy, couple this with a definite action plan to make it a reality. Read and reread the Financial Fitness chapter until the PPF formula becomes a part of you, and how you can create a wealthy mindset even if you don't have much money – endeavour to introduce the wealth creating ideals from the whole of the PLB Code into your own thinking.

As you do this, you'll realise an important thing about abundance, and that is: everything you desire surrounds you – you just need to become good at tuning in to it, and then be focused and relentless in pursuing what you want for yourself. Visualising your desire – seeing it in your mind's eye, is a positive thing, but on its own will not produce results – it's just one part of the process.

If you have an idea of what your dream home would be like, and it's bigger and grander than anything you've experienced in your life to date, then visualising yourself already in that home would be a positive and motivating place to start. The next step would be: what would you have to do and what kind of person would you have to become to make living in a home such as that a reality? What kind of person already lives in a place like that?

Similarly, if there's a dream car you would like to own, then see yourself driving it – and ask yourself the same questions: what would you have to do and what kind of person would you have to become to drive that type of vehicle? What kind of person already drives a vehicle like that?

The same process applies with the type of partner you'd like.

Always view your desires with positive emotions. Create a feeling of excitement whenever you run one of these 'ideal-life' movies through your mind. Get excited, get inspired and get passionate! This will lead to the feeling of inner knowing that what you desire can be yours if you keep up the commitment and the determination.

Thinking about your ideal is about flow and ease not grabbing and grasping. Even though your desires already surround you, they won't become visible to you until you relax and let go, so take the softer route to your desires and avoid creating resistance.

# Twenty-Four Top Tips For Abundance

1. Appreciate all money that comes your way, however small the amount. Appreciate a penny that you find on the floor as much as receiving a large payment.

2. Pay your bills willingly. For example, when you receive your gas or electricity bill, settle it without any resentment – see it as squaring-up for services rendered.

3. Visualise your ideal future knowing that it's

possible. Get excited about what you want in your future. Affirm that things are going your way and your best days are ahead.

4.  Be mindful of ways in which you can boost your vibration at any time: exercising vigorously, getting out into the countryside, bombarding your mind with positive thoughts, etc.

5.  Create a habit of always looking for the positive in all situations – there always is one.

6.  Engage in creative activities that allow you to connect with your true self. Maybe you play a musical instrument, or draw or paint?

7.  Take great care of your body – your temple: exercise, nutrition and rest.

8.  Create a harmonious environment by de-cluttering your life. Get organised, get streamlined – travel light!

9.  Do more of the things that you love – those things that give you great pleasure but may not be understood by others.

10. Trust your inner guidance – that inner knowing, that gut feeling that sixth sense, it's there for a reason.

11. Read uplifting stories and articles – those that give hope and strength.

12. Dress your best at all times, and put your best foot forward at every opportunity – even if you're not the best-looking you can still look your best.

13. Spend time with energetic, uplifting and supportive people ... your high vibration will be positively enhanced.

14. Show gratitude for all the good stuff that's already in your life: feeling healthy, having a roof over your head, having food on the table, living in a safe environment – these are a few places to start.

15. Give thanks for what you don't yet have ... but really long for – that dream you've been working on for years producing results, maybe.

16. Ask the universe for opportunities, and be bold when they arrive and follow up with action.

17. Never dwell on or complain about the past. Close the door, the past no longer exists. Live in the present and plan for the future.

18. Focus on seeing money as a beautiful thing that enhances your life and then brainstorm the many ways that it could enter your world; visualise multiple streams of income: from a job, a business, savings, investments, etc.

19. Move away from the naysayers and the energy drainers. You don't need their infection – keep your distance.

20. See yourself as a money magnet – it flows to you with ease. Imagine turning your annual income into your monthly income. Contemplate having great wealth, and get excited about it; see it, feel it!

21. Be mindful of your thoughts – catch and correct yourself if you find you're dwelling on someone or something that's not energising.

22. Acknowledge the bright side of life as often as you can so that it expands in your life.

23. Don't recognise any problem – always think of the solution.

24. Think of what value you could bring to the marketplace to increase your abundance. What skills and qualities do you have that make you valuable? What new skills and qualities could you acquire to increase your value?

If you follow these twenty-four abundance tips, you'll be living your life as an excuse-free attractor who says yes to life.

# Creating Real Wealth

One of the chief aims of the PLB Code is to encourage people to work towards creating a wealthy mindset.

This is different to just being rich. A lottery winner can be rich, but that doesn't mean they're necessarily wealthy in terms of their attitude, health, friendships, respect for money and enjoyment of life; in fact, they may well be motivated only by greed. I would define a wealthy mindset as one which encompasses the above attributes and can be created from the Code, and as you become stronger, it can be used to fuel your passions, dreams and goals; using knowledge, determination and persistence as components of your strategy for the approach. Undoubtedly money is an important and welcome by-product of this higher-level way of thinking, but only one part. If it's financial freedom that you really want to create in your life, though, you'll need to take a wealthy person's approach when it comes to the way you handle money – you need a wealthy person's philosophy. If you're someone who has a large chunk of month left at the end of your money, maybe it would be wise to look closely at how and on what you're spending. There's a mindset for creating financial wealth and a mindset for blocking financial wealth.

# Mindset Of Poor Thinking

Spending habits: buying unnecessary and often cheap items.

People who indulge in poor thinking have often become so because of the way they've been brought up. They're living within the confines of an inherited mindset. They've learnt poor ways of earning money and handling money – believing it to be scarce and hard to come by. Often what they do get they spend on things they don't really need or are of a low quality or value. It can be anything from the latest and biggest TV with the full package of sports channels and films, to cigarettes, lottery tickets and scratch cards. Some of these people are very hard-working but don't necessarily make their money work hard for them; however, they don't have to live by the bad habits absorbed from the environment in which they were brought up. If they exercise independent thought, they'll be more able to change poor decision-making to decisions that generate wealth.

All the time they're seeing themselves as victims and are not expecting to ever possess substantial amounts of cash, those thoughts will create their reality. I once heard a very disempowering comment expressed by a lady in her 80s while she was watching a TV programme on exotic holidays; she said, "It's only for the b****y rich – it's not for the likes of us." I got the impression that she saw anyone with money as being of a different breed with some preordained right to financial wealth. In reality, though, anyone can increase their financial wealth by challenging and changing their thinking: moving away from the belief that they can only earn money by the hour in a job. There's nothing wrong with having a job, they can often give you a firm foundation in money and experience, keeping you solvent while you explore other ways of creating, and increasing income. You just need to stay open and receptive to ideas and often think outside the box, and if you have a grand vision, seeing it as being more than just a pipe dream.

## Mindset Of 'Middle' Thinking

Spending habits: buying liabilities, believing them to be assets.

People who are 'middle' thinkers often have well-paying jobs, and if they're a couple with two large incomes, they undoubtedly feel quite affluent with an above-average amount of disposable income at the end of each month. The problems begin when they start buying liabilities (things that take money out of your pocket). They move to a bigger house. They buy a top-of-the-range car ... each! They have more than one exotic holiday per year. They consider buying a boat and fitting the house out with every gadget and gizmo on the market, and are forever maxing-out their credit cards. They'll tell you how their house is their biggest asset (assets put money into your pocket) ... but this is only true in certain circumstances. The way I see it, the real owner of the house is the bank with whom you have your mortgage ... they're the ego-free, silent owners while you're the noisy, bragging tenants, and they give you permission to call yourself the owner all the time you're giving them money. As long as you keep crossing their palm with silver they'll happily stay quiet.

A house becomes an asset if you buy it and rent it out and make some profit, because it will then put money back into your pocket, but if you're living in it and paying for it out of your own money, then it's a liability. Years ago, I lived close to a university and I used to regularly rent rooms to students, and I was very aware of how my house would drift from being an asset to a liability, from a liability to an asset, depending on whether I had anyone staying.

Saying that, I do believe that home ownership is a fundamental step towards creating affluence, because let's face it, all the time you're renting you're making someone else affluent. When you do buy, though, I believe it's wise to purchase a property you can comfortably afford; otherwise, it may cause you problems further down the road. Of course, there are many other benefits to owning your own house such as, setting up your own home office, and providing you with a place of rest and sanctuary – it can also act as a psychological foundation in your life, providing you with an inner feeling of comfort and strength.

# Mindset Of Wealthy Thinking

Spending habits: buying assets: property, businesses, stocks, bonds, education.

Wealthy thinking people seem to be operating from a higher place than poor thinkers and 'middlers'. They have a 'prosperity consciousness' which in simple terms means that they never question the abundance that's present in their lives. Many, although not all, happily take full responsibility for themselves, blaming no one else for any failures they experience and viewing those failures positively, as stepping stones to success. You won't find them buying lottery tickets or scratch cards or pulling the handles of slot machines. They're too busy feeling gratitude for the blessings they have in their lives, appreciating the abundance that surrounds them and building their futures by creating rather than competing. Their minds are not preoccupied with thoughts of security because they know that it does not exist; instead, they're just being.

They expect to be financially wealthy and behave accordingly, doing the things that build this wealth, such as buying assets. Their money goes into rental properties, commercial properties, businesses, stocks, bonds, and into creating products that give returns by way of royalties: books, DVDs, commissions, celebrity endorsements etc. They bring value and service to the marketplace. The result is they end up getting paid even while they sleep by creating these multiple streams of income.

They're self-reliant and independent thinkers who make things happen regardless of their circumstances, focusing on what they can control and ignoring what they can't; often acting in the face of fear, leaving all the anxiety, worry and doubt to the poor thinkers and the middlers.

It's often an all-consuming vision for their lives that drives them, almost to the point of healthy obsession, giving them a definiteness of purpose and leaving no time for drifting. This higher thinking leads them to quality behaviours which, coupled with their constant leaning towards action, leads them to top-level results and the realisation of their dreams.

These wealthy thinkers admire the success of others and actively seek out and associate with other positive, results-driven people, who focus on opportunities rather than obstacles. They take their financial advice from other wealthy-thinking people who can help them manage their money well.

They see themselves as bigger than their problems, are always willing to learn and are always looking for ways of making their money work hard for them.

# Picking Up A Penny

Would you pick up a penny? If you answered with a resounding *yes*, then you're likely to be in possession of a very positive life trait – an abundance mindset! To me, picking up a penny shows that you're 'living above zero' and you welcome the small token as a positive sign of abundance even though it doesn't have much value in real terms.

We know that abundance is all around us, if we wish to tune into it and so is scarcity if that's what you're conditioned to see, but let's focus on the abundance because that feeling will cause your vibration to resonate at a higher frequency than one of lack, and the great thing about the higher frequency is that it attracts people of a similar vibration thus keeping you in a positive loop.

Pulsating at a higher frequency opens doors for you; it will allow you to see that your passions and dreams are possible. You'll see the world as a place with great people to meet, great places to go ... amazing experiences to have, so if you're seeing scarcity and lack, zoom out and look at the bigger picture – refocus!

Get out there and try new things and have fun while doing it – be relaxed about failing, laugh it off and get back up and try again. Get comfortable about giving your time, your knowledge, your experience, your money ... your love!

As you view life through a bigger lens, your awareness will grow and you'll understand that on a planet with billions of people there will always be opportunities.

If you're unemployed, you know that there will always be jobs and other ways of earning money. If you don't succeed at an interview, for example, it may illicit negative emotions, especially if you have rent, a mortgage or other bills to pay, but if you work on developing the positive strategies in your life; making yourself stronger, knowing your situation is not permanent, you can be sure you'll survive, and if you make yourself more valuable to the marketplace, and avoid any behaviour that projects desperation or neediness, then with determination and persistence you'll be in a stronger position to be successful when new opportunities arrive.

If you're single, you know that there will always be chances to meet a new a partner, so if you've been let down and have lost someone you really cared for, it may well seem like the end of the world, especially if you felt strongly that they were 'the one', but as the world moves on, you'll surely feel the touch of the healing hand of time, and as you regain your former mojo, you may once again feel the joy and excitement of dating again.

In the meantime ... is that a penny on the floor...??

# Teaching Children About Money

- You can never start too early when it comes to teaching children about money. The sooner you can make them aware of the importance of it in their lives the better. Plant the seeds early that money stays where it's welcomed – it's treasure and must treated with respect.

- Teach them that if they're careful with money and allow it to accumulate, they'll be able to buy some of the things that they love, such as toys, sweets and games.

- Encourage them to get excited about saving their money. When I was a child my parents gave me a red money box with a comic face on it – I named it Bert. The mouth doubled as a slot through which I could 'feed' him with coins. I think all kids should be given a container of some kind so they can have their own mini-bank. As I grew older, I progressed to a large sweet jar which I thought was even better because I could now see the money accumulating inside. So make being money-wise fun, by giving them a container and encouraging them to give it a name, whether it be the name of a person or a descriptive name: I called my sweet jar my Prosperity Pot; a friend called his a Jingle Jar.

- After teaching them how to save, and how to make money accumulate, it's time to teach them how to spend it wisely. Help them understand the difference between their needs, wants and wishes for the future: instead of giving them pocket money and letting them do whatever they want with it, teach them my PPF formula so they allocate some for savings, some for necessities (slightly older children) and some for spending.

- Set them goals and targets for saving. This goes back to making it fun – show them how they can be winners in the money game by making their money work hard for them.

- When it's time to progress from the Prosperity Pot or Jingle Jar, let them have a bank account so they can really see how the principle of compound interest works. Help them to understand about long-term planning; how they can build a foundation for their whole lives by being smart now.

- Take them shopping and teach them to look for value – although not at the cost of quality (false economy isn't saving) – and to keep receipts, encouraging them to establish a sense of control over how their money moves.

- Encourage them to earn money and that there's no such thing as 'something for nothing' – money is a reward for service and value.

- Reward them for good practice and wise money management.

- Discuss shrewd spending decisions. Encourage them to see themselves and their money as being too good and too valuable for gambling.

- Teach them the pitfalls of borrowing and paying interest.

- Teach them about credit cards and debit cards and how they can be wonderful things if used correctly.

- Give regular feedback.

- Don't accept any excuses for poor money decisions (ensuring any feedback and advice you give them is constructive) – encourage complete responsibility.

# The PPF Formula
## (My Three-Way Approach To Handling Money)

1.  **P**ay yourself first

2.  **P**ay your bills

3.  **F**reedom money

It's a great idea whenever you receive money to follow the above formula. Adopting it as a positive money-management strategy can be very beneficial to your financial health. I've been using it since 1994 and it works!

**Paying yourself first** is your number one priority. It's not important how much you can afford to pay yourself – it's the principle of the practice rather than the detail, and ensuring the habit becomes part of your financial routine. Before you pay your utility bills, the credit card company/ies or anyone else, put what you can afford into savings and investments and it will build your future, especially if it's invested wisely and grows even while you're sleeping. Keep some where you can access it easily in case of emergencies – this can act as your 'safety net' money giving you peace of mind. Also, keep some for any educational needs which will be a good investment for your future.

In the past, I've been fascinated how I could invest money and feel pleasure seeing it grow – it was because I found it empowering! It was as if every pound I invested was like another brick being added to the walls of my palace; it was building a wonderful future, yet someone else would choose to take that same amount of money and visit a betting shop and risk it on horse racing ... insane! This, to me, was like tearing a brick down from the walls you already have, and with every loss the walls would get smaller and smaller until they were no more, and eventually the foundations would disappear too – and you'd end up staring into an empty hole in the ground wondering what happened.

Paying yourself first is a habit that builds your future, and its effects will be visible in every area of your life, from your confidence, to your relationships, to your fitness levels – always remember that money is a freedom facilitator! Paying yourself first is the number one step on the road to sound financial practice. Many people, especially the young, spend money in the following order: having fun, paying their bills and lastly, if this happens at all, saving and investing; and they wonder why they end up with a lifetime of struggle.

# "Money is a freedom facilitator."

© 2013 NJT

After you've put away that magic first percentage to build your future, it's now time to:

**Pay your bills.** Now, I'm not one of those people who believes that credit cards are a bad thing; in fact, I think that if you use them wisely they're an amazing tool – as long as you remember that you're in charge of the cards and not the other way round – try to make sure that you pay them off in full every month; you don't want to be paying interest to the credit card companies; that money is better off in your pocket, not theirs.

Paying your bills is a much better and more stress-free way of living – it's the smart and intelligent way. Endeavour to make as many as possible of your financial transactions automatic: set them up so that what you want to invest goes straight out of your current account into a savings account without you having to worry about it. Pay your main utility bills by direct debit and always have any credit cards set to be paid the minimum payment automatically, so you don't incur any late payment fees because of an oversight.

The third step is:

**Freedom money** – what is freedom money? This is the guilt-free money that you can spend in any way that you want – you've invested some, you've covered your bills and now your mind is clear. There's an item of clothing you really fancy, it's quite expensive but if your freedom money covers it then what's the problem? You're in a bar and you buy your friends a round of drinks – it comes to more than you'd really like to spend but if it's covered by your freedom money, then so what!

Money can buy you happiness insofar as – it can remove a lot of the stress and worry from your life, giving you the freedom to pursue your passions. It can take you on holiday to Las Vegas ... but don't put any money in those slot machines.

# Money Can Buy Happiness

I really hate it when I hear people say, "Money can't buy happiness." The reason is that it's such an inaccurate generalisation made mainly by people who don't have much. Sure if you're a great age, in great pain and in poor health, giving you a large sum of money wouldn't really help; or if you've suffered a bereavement and lost a loved one, it's not going to bring the person back or make the hurt go away; but let's say you've been struggling for many years to get ahead, only to be knocked back time and time again, and suddenly you receive an inheritance that clears your mortgage, allows you to park a Ferrari on your drive and to take your holidays in the Maldives. Believe me, you're going to be feeling more than a little bit smiley! Like the proverbial child in the sweetshop your happiness quotient is likely to go through the roof. It's all relative to your wants and needs and desires, and if it's money that allows for these to be realised, then it's money, as an outside stimuli, that pushes your psychological happy buttons. Put simply, money activates your happiness!

Now, I'm not saying it's only material things that make us feel happy; sometimes it's just having things that we love going on in our lives, that signify progress, growth and success, that create it – it could be having an attractive partner, a healthy family, career progression, exploring new places, taking on new challenges, feeling loved ... or even small things that create variety, such as regular trips to the theatre and cinema or dining out with friends. It's the being able to do these things that can foster great happiness and wellbeing, and proves that having and using money in a way that suits you as an individual can provide happiness.

# Financial Fitness Action Invitation

Below are vital ingredients that when added to all the other ingredients in the PLB Code mixing bowl, and worked on consistently, will lead you towards being the excuse-free success you've always wanted to be. It's about creating daily disciplines of action to create momentum.

Decide to:

- Learn as much as possible about abundance and how it surrounds us.

- Work at creating a wealthy mindset, but understanding that money is just one component (you don't have to be rich to be wealthy).

- See money as a life lubricator, that makes your wheels turn smoothly.

- See a penny on the floor as a token of abundance sent your way.

- Take every opportunity to encourage children to see money as treasure that builds their future.

- Introduce the PPF formula as a catalyst for sound money management – always pay yourself first, pay your bills second and enjoy what's left.

- Look for ways of making more money by making yourself more valuable to the marketplace.

- Look for ways of making more money by focusing on the exciting options it gives you.

- Be relaxed about giving money – knowing that even a small contribution to a worthy cause can make a big difference.

# Chapter 6

## THE PLB CODE

# FUN FITNESS

Ye Olde Scroll

LEISURE &
PLEASURE

THE STUDENT

# Creativity

**What better way to put your stamp on life than through your creativity. That wonderful facility we all have to present something to the world that's special and unique to us. Creativity is part of our being and can be an amazing and fun way of bringing out something that lives on the inside.**

It can be released in so many ways depending on the individual, through music, painting, writing, dancing, acting, photography, hair dressing, fashion design and many others – it can be used to express thoughts, feelings and ideas.

Some people have a way of taking something old, and fusing it with new concepts to create something fresh and unique, bringing into existence something that only resided previously in the realms of imagination.

My own experiences with creativity have come through writing this book and through my many years as a songwriter. There have been occasions, for example, where I would start work, writing and producing a song at 9am and would still be sitting there at midnight on the same project, with nothing more than a few short breaks in between, and where I would be so absorbed by it that I'd have to almost force myself to go to bed.

It was as if time took on a different meaning, a different dimension – I never got bored or fatigued, I just loved what I was doing, completely relaxed and at ease creating something amazing out of thought and a vision – I was just being!

When creativity is flowing, even money becomes secondary, as the primary reward is the creativity itself. This way of living makes life stimulating and fulfilling, exciting and fun, where your mind is challenged and originality is embraced. It expands our perceptions –

allows for new ways of problem solving; in fact, those who engage in creativity on a regular basis become properly tuned into life – the connection is made to your true human essence – it's about being authentic.

We all have different ways of being creative, even to the extent that we don't always understand someone else's creativity. I often found this with my songwriting – something that came quite easily to me – in that some people would ask me, "How do you write a song and which comes first, the music or the lyrics?" They couldn't grasp the idea that it came from imagination and knowledge combined and channelled, and that there was no set formula to whether the music came first or the lyrics. To them, the fact that it wasn't something they could see or touch meant they were confused as to where it came from. It wasn't that they weren't creative themselves; it was just that their own creativity was from a different sphere altogether. I'd often attempt to explain it by comparing it to clay on a potter's wheel. Firstly, as you mould and work the clay, you may not see anything at all, but after a while, as you keep working it, you'll see the shape appear of what you're attempting to create; you don't have to search for it: in a way, you just guide it and 'feel it' into existence, and it's the same with a song.

Whenever we can we should take time to express our creativity, as it gives us a chance to really connect with who we are, and what's more, it's always a lot of fun!

# Newness

Purposefully seeking out new experiences in life can be empowering, life-enhancing, exciting and fun as long as they're stimulating and challenging and don't negatively affect anyone else. I like to describe it as planting seeds of discovery in the rich soil of intention.

If you can journey through life maintaining that child-like fascination with all that surrounds you, and carry it into your senior years, then you may get older but you'll never become 'old'.

It really links back to the saying about variety being the spice of life. If you feel that you're reaching an age where you haven't done as much as you'd have liked, then maybe the time is right for you to give close scrutiny to what it is that would really make your heart sing – and take action to make that happen.

There are more opportunities these days than in previous decades to become involved in different activities and to discover new hobbies – and they don't have to be expensive: for example, if you've always fancied singing, it's easy to find a choir to join; if you want to learn a new language, there are adult education courses and many online resources that can help you. Of course, some things may be more for those who have money, such as going on safari or a luxury cruise, but most people can access snorkelling or getting out in the country, going horse riding, taking up chess, reading Shakespeare, making exotic cocktails, visiting the theatre, the cinema or a comedy club; the list is endless.

I personally like to use the start of a new year as a marker to move into the next chapter in my life; it represents a completely fresh start: I'm entering different territory where new discoveries can be made. I've always found it a positive and fun approach to take, in which to leave behind the old year that has been spent and used up, and to go forward with a montage of exciting pictures in my mind, offering hope and encouragement for the year ahead.

We can seek new things or view old things with different eyes and a new understanding by cleaning the lens of our outlook. Never allowing the trials of life to smother the flames of our inner fire – keeping that childlike curiosity, imagination and excitement alive, and by doing this our lives can remain a joy and an adventure well into our senior years.

# "Plant seeds of discovery in the rich soil of intention."

© 2014 NJT

## Happiness From Inside
### ... With Outside Help

I remember as a child my friend Mike coming round. He used to love coming to our house because if you walked down to the bottom of the garden and climbed over the fence, you entered another world. It was in fact a farm and the farm buildings that backed on to our garden were not used that much, which meant that they became an amazing playground where wonderful adventures could be had. There were a couple of large water tanks that had been stored alongside the sheds – these, in our young creative minds became mini-submarines ... and we were the captains! I would climb into one and Mike into the other, and we'd use our imaginations to mimic the sounds that we believed would be heard in real submarines and pretend to send messages to each other of when to dive, when to surface or what to avoid, such as a giant octopus or man-eating sharks. We were so happy, so excited, just being children practising possibility thinking. We'd stepped into a fantasy world created in our imaginations – there was no need for money, no need for permission, no need for searching; we were in the moment, just being – being happy!

We'd found our happiness in our 'now' moments – just making the best of what was around us. When we climbed into those tanks, we *were* the captains of submarines, those sticks *were* periscopes and those imaginary sharks *did* have sharp teeth. We were in awe, full of wonder with no concept of waiting or searching for happiness – we were just being natural!

# "Create 'wow' moments in your 'now' moments."

© 2003 NJT

It's a strange phenomenon that we as adults can actually learn so much from children. They seem to have this amazing ability to become totally absorbed in whatever they focus their energies on, whether it's a ball game, drawing a masterpiece, running an Olympic race in the back garden ... or being the captain of a submarine – the present moment is where it's at and don't they know it!

As we get closer to adulthood, somehow we seem to lose our way. Our conditioning and experiences teach us how to be serious and self-conscious, robbing us of our personal power. In fact, we may, through fearful thinking, become masters of postponement, procrastinators if you like, and start putting off doing the things that give us the greatest pleasure and happiness. We may start developing erroneous beliefs about happiness lying somewhere in the distant future and that we have to earn it or suffer and struggle for it before we can experience it. What madness!

Often when we hear so-called experts talk about happiness; they talk of it only coming from within and not from outside ourselves. I believe that this is right

... but as I mentioned in the Financial Fitness chapter, I also believe that it often requires outside stimuli to activate it.

The gift of happiness resides in our hearts – it's something we're born with, but as we grow older we tend to look at it in different ways; we understand that what we enjoyed as children was a different thing – a childish, naive, innocent form of happiness where the concept of money or sex or other motivators of adults didn't exist or weren't relevant. Even though it can be a positive thing to carry that childlike innocence and inquisitiveness throughout life, the fact is, as adults we need something more. It's true that we can choose to be happy whenever we want, but we can't create the real happy highs that come about through external stimulators or arousers – we need our most powerful and happy states activated from outside. Even though some of these may be very short-lived, this is not always the case, because if, as once again, mentioned in the Financial Fitness chapter, you inherited a large sum of money, let's say, at the age of 55 after struggling all of your life, then the happiness this creates won't necessarily be transient, but could last for many years, even decades.

It's as if we have within us an invisible grid of happy buttons – pleasure buttons, if you like – that can only be pushed from an outside source. All of us have differing banks of buttons – so what makes one person happy can be very different to what makes someone else happy.

Obviously, happiness is the state of mind that we all want to experience as much as possible – it's a place where fear, doubt and hate cease to exist, but we need to receive it with appreciation when it arrives and share its omnipotent glow with others.

# The Rain Storm

I remember one July day in my late teens, clouds had been gathering; we'd had a long hot spell and now it looked as if we were going to pay for it with one hell of a thunderstorm. I could hear the thunder; it sounded as if it was quite some way off ... but then the rain came, yes the rain came – it came down in torrents; warm rain, summer rain. I went downstairs and started to walk through the kitchen, where my brother was standing, towards the back door. He looked at me shocked, "What are you doing?" He was surprised to see me wearing shorts and a t-shirt. "I'm going for a run." "Don't be stupid, have you not seen it out there?" "Yeah, it's gorgeous!" What fun I had as I went running through the warm, refreshing rain ... I got soaked! It was beautiful, what a feeling, what an alive feeling ... a true 'wow' moment!

# Laughter

We all know how infectious laughter can be – when shared in a group, it can envelop everyone under a blanket of joy and fun, bringing people together, increasing happiness, triggering healthy and pleasurable sensations in the body. In fact, laughter can give us a mini-workout, exercising the diaphragm, the abdominal muscles and the shoulders – if you laugh until your sides ache; it's probably a good thing! It's a stress-buster, and like exercise, is a free and easy-to-take 'medicine' that can offer respite from the effects of pain and sadness, helping to take our minds off our troubles, and away from judgements, criticism and doubts – putting distance between us and those thoughts that are a barrier to smiling and laughing.

## 'Joyful Whining'

Many years ago I knew two gentlemen who were both in their late sixties. Joe and George had known each other for a long time and over the years they'd developed a habit of moaning, whining and complaining about anything and everything ... the weather, the economy, the government... but there was something different about Joe and George and that was when they complained they did so from a position of joy, fun and laughter. I remember George said to me once, "We're really serious about not being serious;" this was followed by infectious laughter from the pair of them. They liked to be playful with the absurdities of life and were completely at ease with and accepting of the things that they couldn't control. Often when I went into the bar which these two gentlemen regularly frequented, I would see their smiling faces and hear their infectious laughter. On one particular day, after hearing their totally implausible solution to the problems with the economy, I said, "I've got a name for your regular musings: 'joyful whining', because you always seem to find humour, even in the gravest of events."

I think we can all learn something from Joe's and George's philosophy by understanding that humour and laughter takes us to a higher place: they raise our vibration and increase our attractiveness.

# Public Speaking

If I told you public speaking can be a lot of fun and very good for your health, you'd probably think I was mad. Many would see it as being scary, stressful and anxiety promoting and would certainly not associate it in any way with health or fun.

The reality is that it can benefit you in three ways.

- Firstly, it can be very good for your immune system.

- Secondly, it can generate laughter, and in so doing, increase our level of joy.

- Thirdly, if done on a regular basis, it encourages frequent social contact which promotes longevity.

## The Immune System

We all know that public speaking can be very stressful, causing your heart to beat faster and your blood pressure to rise. Butterflies may start wildly fluttering around in your stomach, but what also happens is the body releases certain chemicals that are mobilised into your blood stream, ready to protect the body by fighting infections and healing wounds. We could, as such, call the effect public speaking has on us 'good stress', as it's fairly mild and soon dissipates after the speech has finished, leaving us, hopefully, on that familiar 'high' of sorts, thinking that the experience wasn't as bad as we thought it would be.

## Laughter Is Medicine

Laughter plays its part in boosting our immune system, because it has a medicinal effect on the body. Much of the 'bad stress' disappears as it creates a relieving effect; clearing away fears and worries that may induce illness. A good, hearty laugh releases natural feel-good endorphins that can be, to a certain extent, morphine-like in relieving pain. It's also beneficial in helping to keep us in that tension-free 'glow-zone' of contentment, where our joy oozes from every pore of our bodies.

## Social Contact

Becoming socially active can be incredibly beneficial to your longevity. People who have regular and consistent contact with others – family, friends, the community, with social groups – tend to live longer, and they're also much more likely to make quick recoveries from illness or injuries. As humans we're wired to connect with others. We just have to be aware that our emotions are an 'open' system that's easily affected by the moods of other people. If the people with whom we associate are fun to be with and laugh a lot, this will definitely have an effect on us.

Many people who are petrified of public speaking often take their first step to overcoming that fear by joining a Toastmasters International club. Check their website to find a club near you; it could be one of the most important decisions you'll ever make, as far as your personal development and wellbeing are concerned. Once there, you'll find a mutually supportive atmosphere comprising a mix of people from different backgrounds, all of whom want to do the same as you: use a safe environment to overcome their fear of public speaking.

If you take the above step, there's every chance your confidence will grow each time you speak, as you learn the tips, tools and techniques for delivering a great talk: it's about what you say, how you say it, and your body language – in a nutshell, creating congruence. If you see yourself as a flower that's never bloomed – this could be your chance.

Make public speaking an indispensable part of your excuse-free, empowered life and you may well find yourself with a healthier immune system, more friends, and more reasons to laugh.

Speak up! It's a confidence building vitamin.

# Travel
## (Expanding The Mind)

Travelling can be a very positive and fun way to expand our minds by giving us opportunities to learn more about the world in which we live – it opens us up to greater understanding. There are so many amazing places to visit and cultures to experience, that would astound us if we could just muster up the courage to get out into the world. I hear you say, "Yeah but... these places are way over my budget." Well, if your budget is a little tight, why not start off visiting places much closer to home? Sometimes we get so engrossed in only focusing on the paradise-like places far away that we fail to see the beauty and value in those places that are close to us.

Whether your destination is near or far, there's no getting away from the fact that travel is like oxygen to the mind – if we live our lives in a restrictive, compressed and closed way, we can end up with all kinds of psychological problems. It can send us stir crazy; it's like living our lives in chains even though we're free.

Often it comes back to excuses once again, to why people don't get out and travel and explore – lack of money, work commitments, family commitments ... even fear of the unknown. All these excuses will lead to one thing – 'The Big Book of Regrets' at the end of your life.

I remember standing in the high street of a town called Alton, in southern England, and having a conversation about travel with someone in his 50s who'd lived in the town all his life. He told me that he would love to visit different places and experience different cultures but his budget wouldn't allow it. I asked him if he'd ever visited the house of the world-renowned English literary giant Jane Austen. He informed me that he hadn't. I suggested that it would be a good place to start as her house was less than two miles away from where we were standing – two miles away from where he'd lived for over 50 years.

Travel can be a veritable life-changer – it can help to make you a happier, more confident and rounded person.

Think of all the great stories you'll be able to tell of the wonderful experiences you've had – just remember, the mind works best when it's fed a powerful smorgasbord of 'mindfood' – emanating from the garden of variety; it doesn't grow from sameness.

Below is an example of how I used travel to freshen my mind after a difficult time in my life.

# The Road To Corpus Christi

We were just coming out of the northern winter, a winter that had been extra cold and dark for me because I'd not long split with my now ex-girlfriend. I really needed a change of scene, some sunshine, some vitamin D to lift me out of my blue funk. My world seemed to be becoming increasingly small and tight – the walls of my multiple comfort zones were moving in ever closer and my mind was beginning to ache from the restriction. This was when I decided that I really needed a break, to get away somewhere new to recharge my batteries – so where would I go? At this time I'd never travelled to the Texas side of the Gulf of Mexico – so I decided to take a few weeks in the city of Corpus Christi ... on my own – I needed time to rediscover me. I flew from London, England to Houston, Texas; I'd booked only one night in a hotel and a rental car for the following day. Taking a steady cruise down to Corpus was part of the fun of the trip. It was April and I was thriving in the hot Houston sunshine; it was the tonic I needed, taking in the music of the busy city, gazing up at the skyscrapers in the centre, where the tallest one appeared to have a green hue as the sun reflected off the glass ... and little wispy clouds lingering near its top.

My mind was now completely off my problems; instead, I was fully engaged in the present moment ... and the near future, anticipating what I might find in Corpus. Would it live up to the claims of being "a secret Miami Beach"? I was about to find out.

My journey down from north Houston, some two hundred and forty miles away, had been very pleasant, if uneventful ... I only stopped twice, once to enjoy a meal of fine Texan beef and once to refuel in the small town of Refugio.

I was pleasantly surprised at how green and flat eastern Texas was ... and how empty the roads were once I'd left the city limits behind; now, as I progressed south my thoughts were completely consumed by Corpus Christi – the jewel in the Texan crown ... supposedly! I remember hearing it described as "the sparkling city by the sea", so as I edged closer and closer along Highway 37 my anticipation grew.

My first port of call was the City Beach area and as I drove over the harbour bridge I was met with a breath-taking panorama in front of me – a glorious view of the whole bay area: the magnificent white sands of the City Beach, the U.S.S Lexington aircraft carrier in the centre, the sparkling azure-blue waters of the Gulf of Mexico and the ubiquitous and majestic Washingtonia palm trees swaying in the breeze. Well, it might not be Miami Beach, but I knew I'd just discovered something special.

I stayed in the beach area for several days, with my visit to the U.S.S Lexington being the highlight. This imposing WWII aircraft carrier preserved as a permanent museum in the bay, was truly a great day out, and I'll always remember standing on the deck and seeing another glorious view of the bay from a different angle: over to the left was the building that gives Corpus Christi its identity – the Bank of America, an impressive structure dominating the skyline; to the centre was the harbour bridge; and to my right the near-deserted City Beach; and all bathed in glorious sunshine... Wow! I must have spent over an hour rooted to the spot drinking in this cool scene.

The following day, I decided to visit the Texas State Aquarium situated nearby, and after viewing the giant turtles and sharks I got talking to a couple called Greg and Carrie from Dallas – we had a lot in common, and they were as keen to hear about my life in England as I was their lives in Texas. Before saying our goodbyes, they invited me to join them for a seafood lunch the following day. How could I say no? A place and a time were fixed.

The next morning I set out to drive across the city to Mustang Island, which is connected to Corpus Christi by a causeway. On reaching the island I was left open-mouthed by the amazing and beautiful white sandy beaches. I drove the length of the island to the small Town of Port Aransas on the northern tip before deciding to head back for my lunch appointment. It wasn't long after joining Highway 358 heading back into the city, that I noticed my red Chevrolet was starting to make some odd noises, and with the subsequent deterioration in the car's performance and the smell of burning rubber, I realised what had happened – I had just had a blow-out on one of my rear tyres. I guided the car over to the hard shoulder and climbed out into the midday heat to inspect the damage – the right rear tyre was ripped to shreds, but instead of being negative, I thought, "that's quite an impressive blow-out; I'll take some photos to show the folks back home." I then proceeded to hold an impromptu photo shoot right there on the hard shoulder as trucks and cars thundered past me – my only regret was I never did make that lunch appointment with Greg and Carrie...

As my days in Corpus Christi glided past, I kept thinking the same thoughts: "What a great way to exorcise the blues. What a great way to refresh your mind: getting out into the world; getting out in the sun." It was medicine for the soul. As I prepared to head off along Highway 35, Houston bound ... I knew I'd definitely fallen in love. This place was without doubt an undiscovered Miami Beach but with a character all of its own. Bit of a rough diamond you might say ... but a great place to visit! I enjoyed the people and their generous hospitality, boosted my vitamin D levels no end, energised my spirit and had a whole lot of fun.

I kept glancing in my rear-view mirror at the city skyline as it grew increasingly smaller behind me, and I thought to myself, to paraphrase Arnold Schwarzenegger : "I'll be back!"

# Giving Back

Giving back is increasingly being seen as an important component in a well-rounded person's life – it's a key ingredient in a meaningful life where contribution plays an important role in your mindset.

It's about looking beyond the selfish me, me, me attitude of material possessions and self-aggrandisement and opening up and sharing time, money and/or resources for the greater good.

A profound sense of this is when we're able to affect positive change, for example with regards: wildlife preservation, protecting the oceans and the forests, helping people in poorer countries have better sanitation, or perhaps something more close to home such as helping those in our own community who are less well off than us.

I believe we have an inbuilt faculty towards wanting to make a difference – it's something that stirs in our souls – but we need to find the best channel for our contribution. It helps if it's connected to a passion we have, something which moves us emotionally.

The best place to start would be with engaging your imagination, and considering your own skills and how they could best be utilised. If you don't have spare money that you can contribute, then think of other ways: your time, your organisational skills, your physical strength, your drive and energy.

It can feel freeing and empowering to know that you're successfully trading time that may have otherwise been used to watch mindless TV programmes or aimlessly surf the net, for something imminently more valuable. It's a great feeling when you do a good deed for someone and you know that what you did made a real difference to them – if only you could bottle that feeling!

Let, "How can I help? How can I be of service?" be your mantra as you take time to sit and ponder what contribution, what legacy you would like to leave.

# Fun Fitness Action Invitation

Below are vital ingredients that when added to all the other ingredients in the PLB Code mixing bowl, and worked on consistently, will lead you towards being the excuse-free success you've always wanted to be. It's about creating daily disciplines of action to create momentum.

Decide to:

- Work on your creativity, and if you haven't discovered what it is yet; try different things, you may surprise yourself.

- Take every opportunity to try new things, to remove some of the 'sameness' from your life, and you'll never be bored.

- Celebrate every 'now' moment – learn from the past, live in the present and build for the future.

- Laugh and laugh often. Mix with people who spread joy, watch TV programmes that resonate with your sense of humour. Do things you love.

- Use the unlikely medium of public speaking to mix socially – join a club – it can be a lot of fun, especially if you feel there's a secret, undiscovered 'stand-up comedian' inside you.

- Travel as often as you can afford. It can be fun and interesting to meet different people and see different places.

- Have fun giving back. It can be very satisfying to contribute, to do something that has a positive effect on others.

---

# Chapter 7

---

# THE RESOURCEFUL STATE OF MIND— NO EXCUSES!

## THE GRANDMASTER

"The stage is set— step up and let the show begin."

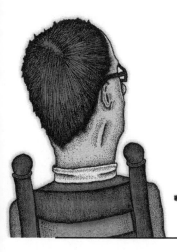

## THE STUDENT

# Time And Action

**The clock is ticking – it's relentless, never stopping for anything or anyone. We have a clear choice, we can use our time wisely or we can waste it or kill it. Using it wisely gives us strength and hope for when we're older whereas wasting it will only wreck our future.**

One of the craziest statements I hear people make is, "I like to be busy, because it makes the time go quicker." Why would any sane person want to make the time go quicker? Never talk of valuable time in the negative!

It doesn't matter what we do, we can never slow or stop the march of time, but we can use it productively and march with it so that where we're heading proves to be somewhere desirable.

It's strange how our concept of it changes as we get older. When we were kids it would go slow – a term at school seemed never ending – but as we get older it seems to speed up at a frightening rate, which emphasises the importance of planting 'seeds of success' when you're young, so that when you're older you can enjoy a bountiful harvest. Now, I'm not saying it's ever too late. In fact, I firmly believe that any time spent planting positive seeds for your future is time well invested, but obviously, the earlier you do it the more time you have to enjoy the harvest.

My advice would be not to waste a moment in planting those time-sensitive seeds. Reduce the amount of TV you watch and/or video games you play, and you could have a bright future waiting up ahead. The opposite only guarantees that you'll end up reading from 'The Big Book of Regrets'.

Always think how valuable your future is to you – and then think how valuable your time is now.

# "Stop killing time – start filling time with productive activity."

© 2014 NJT

Bring on the 'A' word – it's time for Action! It's business time! Be courageous, set your standards high and become accountable for those standards – it shows you're taking the project of you and your future seriously. Don't lose time waiting for things to be perfect; they never will be. Take your first step right now, and you can handle any problems as they arise. The desire to act is at its strongest when you first have it, so waste no time in letting its force guide you.

Take action, and all fear will melt away. A good example of this is when you're preparing to speak in public – without doubt the scariest, most nerve-wracking part is the waiting just before you go on, but if you've done your preparation, chances are once you get out there in front of the audience your nerves will dissipate, and afterwards you'll likely wonder how and why you felt so nervous before you began.

## Circus School

I often look at working on the strategies of the PLB Code as an act of juggling with many balls – it's like a visit to circus school: it can be dynamic, colourful, fun and above all ... challenging! When you become skilled in its application you'll be surprised how easy it really is...

If you look up at the tight-wire – the performer makes it look so easy; look at the person on the walking globe – it seems so effortless; but it wasn't that long ago that these guys were taking their first tentative and shaky steps towards mastering their particular disciplines.

How many falls were experienced, how many unproductive thoughts overcome, before mastery of the walking globe became natural? How many baby steps were taken on a practice tight-wire, only three feet from the ground, before enough confidence and competence were gained to carry the performer from one side of the ring to the other, at a great height, with ease?

Maybe you see your life as a combination of balancing and juggling – so many balls to be kept in the air at the same time while you try to avoid wobbling and falling off of your unicycle – you doubt whether you'll ever master it, but look at the jugglers – look at how easy they make it appear. If they can do it, so can you!

What it really boils down to is how much you really want the victory, and the prizes and rewards that go with living a fabulous life. When you want it as much as you want your next breath, then and only then will you start to make extraordinary progress. When you make that decision to play for real, all sorts of seemingly random events will pop up in your life to help you and guide you. Show commitment, perseverance, discipline, passion and enthusiasm. Let your mission consume you – become that student of success.

Always remember the best way to go is one small step at a time.

## Quick Start

Now we've read through the disciplines of the five PLB Code areas for balance-awareness we need to get started on our journey to becoming a stronger, more focused, excuse-free version of ourselves and create that resourceful state of mind. We need to break it down and just take one step in each area as a place to begin...

## Mental Fitness – The Control Centre
#### let's be positive to people (Consistently)

## Physical Fitness – The Vehicle
#### let's take time to exercise (Today)

## Relationship Fitness – Your Connections
#### let's nurture our friendships (With love)

## Financial Fitness – The Oil
#### let's invest some money (However small)

## Fun Fitness – Leisure And Pleasure
#### let's remember to laugh! (Often)

# A Snapshot
## (Of Someone Who Has Successfully Implemented The PLB Code Into Their Life)

Someone, who has successfully implemented the Positive Life-Balance Code into their life as a key component for their personal development, would be seen first and foremost as an individual who wishes to make the most of their brief but precious time on this planet. They're not looking for some unobtainable perfection as the perfect person who doesn't make mistakes, but instead deserve applause for being someone who has made a bold decision to raise the standard in their life.

It's almost as if the Code has given them a light-bulb moment, illuminating a new path by helping them tap into a greater awareness – satisfying a longing they have inside to take their life to a new level.

Mentally, they come across as being calm and serene – liking and accepting themselves and liking and accepting others for who they are, and not being overly judgemental or suffering from the unfortunate condition of 'an over-active ego gland'. If you engaged them in conversation, you would more than likely find them open and interesting ... and most importantly, genuinely interested in you. With a sunny disposition reflecting a positive attitude born from a decision to recognise, and show gratitude for, all the good stuff that they have in their lives – they drink fully from the present moment, completely free from any obsessing about the past or the future. They're stable in their environment – optimistic and ambitious, realistic and centred – with no erroneous beliefs that life owes them anything. You'll find them positive most of the time, but accepting of those odd days when their joy takes a little longer to manifest. Not for one moment are they happy with everything that's going on in the world, but they know that being upset about things that they can't control is a pointless and futile way to live. They're at peace with themselves and the world in which they live, joyous in their spiritual awareness.

Often using kind and encouraging words, they're happy to share their time with people. They have strong opinions and always operate with a mind of their own, unswayed by peer pressure no matter who they're with or what they're doing; but they're comfortable listening to and debating with people who have differing opinions, open to criticism without allowing it to unduly affect or direct them – always giving the final say in any situation to the power of their own council.

You can tell by their outward appearance that they take care of themselves with exercise, diet and adequate sleep, with a dress sense that's stylishly original yet appropriate – rarely sloppy or over the top.

If they're in a relationship they're loving and supportive – giving of themselves fully – but comfortable and relaxed if they're not, with an inner knowing that the right person will come along at the right time, so there's no reason to be concerned.

As out-going and sociable people; you may find them at a show or an event, immersing themselves in culture and history. Delighting in the architecture of the big city, but also perfectly at home in the rolling meadows of the countryside, as they love and admire the rhythms of nature – respecting birds, animals, trees, insects and everything about it; always fascinated by its power and beauty.

They're generous in every way with their friends, and would be willing to help out at any time if needed, because they value good friendship. They're quick to forgive but are not walk-overs – kind and friendly but not to be taken advantage of – they don't suffer fools gladly. They're quick to remove themselves from the company of people who are negative and critical, but not without some encouraging words.

They're sensible with money but are still generous – they shop for quality and value and don't spend on frivolous items.

They exude a joyful personality; an open spirit – often laughing at the absurdities of life – they exhibit a sense of fun. They're determined, persistent, cheerfully ambitious ... and very importantly, free from the malady of excuse-making.

# A Resourceful You – No Excuses!

A massive benefit of making the PLB Code a part of your life is, as mentioned in the Mental Fitness area, the stronger you become in all areas the easier it is to handle adversity and the less likely you'll be beaten down by negative people and circumstances.

If, for example, you've been in or are still in a job you hate or in a relationship that has run its course and should really be filed away under 'history and experience', then you may have found your energy and focus being pulled in a direction that doesn't serve you, where your mind starts obsessively replaying related negative events and you become pre-occupied with the pain, with justice and with how unfair it all is. If those that are affecting you become aware that they're twisting your emotions at will, you may end up dancing like a puppet to their tune. You'll find that people will only oppress you when they can see that they're pulling your strings, but when they cease to get a reaction they'll more than likely move on to some other weaker victim.

If you passively tolerate these bad situations you end up surrendering control – basically, giving away your personal power.

However, if instead of enduring such circumstances, you choose to control your mental diet, exercise vigorously and circulate socially, constantly building up your strength, then you'll be stronger all round and tolerating these situations won't be an issue, because you'll be fully able to handle and remedy them with ease. Rather than being passive and letting life happen to you, you'll be in control with your solid foundation of personal power there for all to see.

By directing your life based on the five areas you'll become too strong to allow these detractors to lead you off course, too powerful to be led to their desert of despair. You'll be in possession of a resourceful state of mind which will lead you to a better place. Instead of ending your days reading from 'The Big Book of Regrets', which is nothing more than a solemn treatise from the cul-de-sac of 'if only', where you realise that your whole life was directed by others, instead, you'll have become the author of your 'Big Book of Dreams' – full of essays of exciting times, so I implore you to be bold and to take the decision to move from weakness to strength, from defeat to victory. Make your life a passion play of perfection – and it's never too late – if you're 50 or 60 or more and the first half of your life has been tragic then make what's left magic.

# "Don't let your swan song be the rhapsody of regret."

© 2014 NJT

I want you, for a few moments to imagine yourself at the end of your life … I know it sounds morbid, but think how you would feel if you never did any of the things that you really wanted to do. Maybe you were too immersed in the noise of everyday routine that you never heard the clock ticking, or maybe you just didn't get around to it. Whatever the reason, ask yourself one question: "Is any excuse big enough to justify the fact that you just didn't do it?" Now that you know it's too late – forever! How long is forever? We're all living in a flower garden, so don't be one of those sad people who when asked at the end of their lives, "What did you think of the flowers?" reply, "What flowers?"

# "Don't walk the length of life's garden without admiring and smelling the flowers."

© 2013 NJT

Let us not be martyrs, let us choose to be happy and productive in all of our precious moments, right now, rather than waiting. I've heard it said that if you wait for love, happiness and opportunity, then love, happiness and opportunity will wait for you. Giving ourselves fully to every moment we have will undoubtedly make our journey extraordinary.

Make the commitment, put the strategies to work in your life, be persistent, be determined, and practise, practise, practise – let repetition be the formulator, the master tool in your armoury for reaching the excuse-free higher ground, and you'll have become truly wealthy.

I will leave you now by echoing the sentiment expressed in the famous song by Edith Piaf: "Non, je ne regrette rien." No, I regret nothing ... because I said yes to life and no to excuses.

**I wish you well on your journey.**

## *Neil James Thompson*

## A Stronger Version of You

*Your critics and detractors shrink in size in direct proportion to how big, strong and powerful you become. Those enemies that once appeared like towering giants now appear minute and irrelevant. All because of you ... and how you burnt your excuses on the challenging fires of life, whilst they still carry theirs around, like highly-protected precious stones; treasures of comfort and delusion. They stand weak and annoyed at your lack of interest in them and their opinions, and at how their rocks and arrows bounce off you or are brushed away like soft confetti.*

*You're unrecognisable as the person you once were ... and don't they hate it ... and don't you love it!*

© 2014 NJT

I wanted to include all 21 of my quotations in one place, so using the collective noun of an 'enlightenment', here is:

# Neil's 'Enlightenment' Of Quotations

"If you're thinking negative thoughts about past upsets and hurts – then you're not busy enough working on your dreams."

© 2014 NJT

"Don't make an excuse – make a plan – to make a life."

© 2013 NJT

"An excuse is a 'get-out clause'; the only trouble is some will get you out of a great future."

© 2014 NJT

## "The engine of desire turns the wheels of success."

© 2014 NJT

## "Eagles don't need the approval of turkeys to fly high."

© 2014 NJT

## "Positive self-talk: it puts fire in your belly and steam in your veins."

© 1986 NJT

## "Let's colour up our lives and paint our own rainbows."

© 2003 NJT

## "Our words are like verbal boomerangs – what we throw out there, is what we tend to get back."

© 2003 NJT

## "The higher your self-esteem the easier it is to handle adversity."

© 2013 NJT

**"Confidence is about raising the
banner of faith in yourself."**

© 2014 NJT

**"Enthusiasm is faith and
excitement in advance – born from
the anticipation of something that
inspires and delights you."**

© 2014 NJT

**"Use the desire in your present to
put the promise in your future."**

© 2014 NJT

**"Exercise is an easy-to-take
medicine that always makes you
feel better."**

© 2014 NJT

**"Be aware that your mindset is
always on display, through your
face, voice and body."**

© 2014 NJT

**"Life's too short to be racist."**

© 2014 NJT

---

**"Money is a freedom facilitator."**

© 2013 NJT

---

**"Plant seeds of discovery in the rich soil of intention."**

© 2014 NJT

---

**"Create 'wow' moments in your 'now' moments."**

© 2003 NJT

---

**"Stop killing time – start filling time with productive activity."**

© 2014 NJT

---

**"Don't let your swan song be the rhapsody of regret."**

© 2014 NJT

---

**"Don't walk the length of life's garden without admiring and smelling the flowers."**

© 2013 NJT

# Acknowledgements

To the many people who have helped and encouraged me on my journey in taking this book from an idea to completion, a very special thank you – in particular to:

My parents, Kathleen and Harry Thompson who have always done their very best for me ... and more.

Robert May's school where I was a former pupil – to librarian Paula Ward and head of art Tony Peters for their positive vibes in embracing my project, and encouraging pupil George Gardner to submit examples of his excellent artwork for inclusion in this book.

James McCullen for his unique interpretation of my 'vision' for the Grandmaster and the Student.

Simon Ellinas who supplied three top-notch professional illustrations including the 'Motorbikers' on the front cover.

Abi Truelove for editing this book and challenging some of my generalisations and opinions – leading to a much more polished final product.

Nidrick Publishing visionaries for their enthusiasm, knowledge, and belief in me.

...and finally, to:

The many close friends and acquaintances who have assisted me at my talks and seminars and offered suggestions, opinions (some of which I took on board) and positivity. You've helped make this book what it is today ... you know who you are.

## I applaud you all.

# Artwork Acknowledgements

All artwork concepts: Neil James Thompson

## Illustrations

*Motorbikers*

*Why am I not rich?*

*Joyful Whining*

**© 2014 Simon Ellinas**


*The Grandmaster*

*The Student*

*The Scroll*

**© 2014 James McCullen**


*The Mirror*

*The Smoking Board*

*The Doormat*

*The Flower Garden*

**© 2014 George Gardner**

# Copyrights

www.neiljamesthompson.com